# Financial Management in Hotels

# Financial Management in Hotels

**D.K. SINGH**
*Vice-President*
*Heritage Institute of Hotel and Tourism*
*Agra*

**AMAN PUBLICATIONS**
NEW DELHI

*Published by*
Rajiv Jain for Aman Publications
LG-4A, Ganpati Bhawan,
4675-B/21, Ansari Road,
Darya Ganj, Delhi - 110002
PH: 23255012, 23282127
E-mail: sshjbs@yahoo.com



First Published – 2010

ISBN–81–8204–048-051-5
ISBN–978-81–8204–-051-9



SOLE DISTRIBUTOR
**JINDAL BOOK SERVICES**
LG-4A, Ganpati Bhawan,
4675-B/21, Ansari Road,
Darya Ganj, Delhi - 110002

*Jacket Designed by* :
S.M. Graphics

*Printed by*:
NCT Printers & Publishers, Delhi, India

# Preface

The traditional hotel financial management generally attaches more importance to the accounting management while ignores the regulation management of finance. For example, what some financial managers or financial controllers are often signed and approved by the general manager is handled with all strength whether it is correct or not. Not all the decisions are correct because of the limited ability of human. It is required to ask relevant departments to advise and provide evidences for leaders to make decisions. Therefore, a purchasing list must be signed finally by general manager after department manager and financial controller check and sign. None of them can be missed. Otherwise, fault may take place while making decisions. The financial affairs of hotels attach more importance to financial control than accounting merely. Purchase prices of food and goods should be controlled strictly and the regular market survey should be made by financial controller. It is not allowed to purchase at will without the approval of financial controller. The hotel financial affairs are not merely the work of checking and calculating after "what is done cannot be undone".

Financial department is not the executive body but a management body of the function. So financial management needs to be given re-thinking and positioning. In the development and operation, a set of complete, rigorous and reasonable system has been formed for guidance after repeated breaking-in and operations. We must study conscientiously and learn the knowledge about financial management and management methods from advanced hotels to improve our management system and level.

The internationalization and standardization level of financial management of hotel will also been improved. However, there is still a great gap between overseas and domestic hotels. To narrow the gap, we must make every effort and urge the counterpart of the domestic hotels to establish confidence, at the same time seek for the differentiation to further strengthen the management and uplift the level of internationalization and standardization level of hotel financial management.

The area of financial management is a vital but often inaccessible part of the hotel business. Having the knowledge and the ability to use money properly makes all the difference to the turnover and success of the business. The present book is written specifically for those industry executives who need to be able to decipher, appreciate and utilise valuable financial management tools and techniques in order to realise maximum profits.

Highly practical in its scope and approach, this book outlines the procedure and purpose behind various financial activities, demonstrates how an appropriate analysis of financial reports can drive the business strategy forward from a well-informed base, and highlights the key financial issues one need to consider in a host of decision-making situations. Combining a user-friendly structure with frequent international cases, this book will be ideal for all students of hospitality, as well as a vital source of information for practitioners already in the industry.

**D.K. SINGH**

# Contents

# 1

# Finance and Hotel Industry

Globalisation is a natural outgrowth of trends that have evolved during the past 50 years. International hotel chains were invented after World War II; they grew in the 1960s, and expanded greatly in the following two decades. Industry and economic trends in this decade have further propelled the growth of internationally-oriented hotel companies for a variety of reasons.

Severe overbuilding of hotel markets, particularly in the United States during the 1980s, halted new development almost entirely, while scarcity of growth and development opportunities in markets around the world has further supported the trend toward industry consolidation. Many companies committed to growth have found that opportunities in their back yards have been limited because of overbuilding, and they have been forced to look beyond mature domestic markets to offshore opportunities.

The pressures to expand beyond national boundaries have largely arisen from the need for growing hotel companies to reach 'critical mass'— the point at which a network of properties is sufficiently large to satisfy the travel needs of the hotel company's most valued customers. For different companies with varying products and locations, critical mass will vary in scope.

A hotel organisation, for example, may reach a point in which there is no other viable option than to expand across national boundaries if it wishes to grow, achieve critical mass and benefit from the economies of scale that accompany it. If this is the case, leadership will need to recognise the imperative of organising as a global company.

As an example, consider an international hotel company that is well established in North America and Europe. In today's world market, company leadership may cast attention on the potential for moving into burgeoning Asia/Pacific markets to compete with established regional companies. Companies considering such strategic options can succeed against strong local and regional competitors only if they capitalise on the advantages derived from being a global company.

While the large international chains continue to expand on a global basis, there are in the United States a number of brand names that have yet to reach the critical mass required for marketing success. The question this presents to the industry can be stated simply. Will the demands of globalisation encourage further consolidation as smaller companies that have not achieved critical mass are acquired or put out of business? The need for hotel companies to achieve critical mass and the attendant economies of scale suggests that we will see a diminishing number of larger companies in the future as the imperatives of global expansion persist.

Economies of scale are real, not imagined, and marketing on a global basis creates a significant competitive edge. It is certain that brands and products will be increasingly marketed on a truly global basis. Growth and development functions will thus become even more critical for those organisations that have not yet achieved critical mass.

For those companies pursuing a global strategy and accustomed to hotel management contracts, franchising relationships and non-recourse financing, significant adjustments will need to be made to the growth and development model. In a number of markets around the world, the bifurcation of ownership from management and management from marketing is a concept yet to achieve real maturity. The process that promotes these concepts is a slow one and global-minded companies will need to respond accordingly.

The differences in financing, owning, operating and marketing hotel properties will thus eventually narrow in a more global environment. The challenge for companies growing into markets where local partnerships and alliances are required for success will be to convince their foreign counterparts of the benefits of structures that have been successful in their home countries. A company going offshore with a business concept, however, cannot assume that it will be wholly accepted. Differences will gradually break down, but for the time being it may be necessary to adjust to local realities.

## Global Brand and Products

Hospitality customers increasingly seek predictable services that support their ability to move quickly and easily around the world. Indeed, the businesses and lifestyles of these multi-cultural travelers have themselves been shaped by globalisation. The concept of projecting single brands globally is thus alluring, as well as being fully within the grasp of many hospitality companies. Nevertheless, there continues to be uncertainty about the benefits of establishing a single-brand presence in a global marketplace, in contrast to responding to the unique conditions at the local level.

A number of international hotel companies have sought the economies of scale attendant to developing single brands and products, and providing them in a uniform fashion to as many markets around the globe as possible. A counter-vailing trend is that many people — both tourists and business travelers — seek the unique qualities and customs of an individual locale. In response, some international hotel companies have tried to reflect local culture in the way their hotels are designed and operated.

This is clearly an arena in which there is no one right answer, but rather a balance of complex factors required. For example, there is a general consensus that "global travelers," who travel frequently whether for business or recreation, usually prefer a uniform product, because they want the convenience and comfort of predictability, and they demand a high level of service. Those who travel less frequently, but have a fairly high level of sophistication may avoid such dominant global brand and product concepts. A third group is looking for what they are accustomed to, and are attracted by brands they are familiar with; in essence, they prefer to stay in environments that reflect their home-based experience.

Customer expectations are related to the level of the product, and hotel products at the lower end of the spectrum tend to be easier to standardise globally, in part because these properties are more clearly defined by physical attributes, which can be duplicated. At the upper end of the product quality spectrum, customers seek subtle differences in services and quality, which are not easily replicated.

## GLOBAL HOTEL COMPANIES

For the larger well-established international hotel companies that have circled the world in the quest for new opportunity, globalisation has been a strategic concept for a number of years. International hotel companies have had to confront virtually all of the issues facing global enterprises — and in many cases more. Unlike a manufacturer with an overseas plant, for example, a hotel company must export its entire operating business to function in diverse cultural and geographic settings. Hotel companies must have the capability of establishing an entire business concept in dramatically different local environments.

As the new century approaches, formulating organisational structures that can integrate individual businesses in one seamless global structure will remain an on-going challenge. Information technology clearly is one major factor shaping the opportunities for how global hotel companies organise themselves, offering the ability to communicate with customers electronically and linking far-flung operations.

Global organisations also benefit by becoming flatter, in contrast to pyramid-shaped structures with strong central authority. Such decentralised organisations can narrow the distance between employers and employees, at the same time putting management and staff closer to the customer.

Organisational structures that are based on hierarchical systems with authority centralised at a headquarters location, as a result, may be increasingly obsolete because they distance management from the customer, while at the same time failing to empower line management and staff responsible for delivering services.

Fortunately, "flatter" and more decentralised organisations are greatly facilitated by the increasing sophistication of technology and communications.

In addition, hotel company employees represent a melting pot of cultures, customs and languages, requiring new visioning and management skills to manage effectively, as well as a commitment to education and training that is unprecedented in its breadth. Today's hotel schools will need to increase their focus on issues that have to do with a global environment — communications, international marketing and law, history, social studies, geography and language. Company-wide training in a global organisation to assure consistent leadership, operational skills and service delivery also represents a considerable challenge.

All of these factors suggest that companies expanding globally can benefit greatly by forming strategic alliances. A number of companies are moving towards such alliances with regional partners as a key strategy to provide entry to new and relatively unfamiliar markets and assure a higher level of local knowledge. Going it alone is increasingly expensive and frequently more risky. Substantial sums of money can be spent trying to conquer a region, and there may be considerable wisdom in forging alliances with local and regional partners. Foreign hotel groups have long found it difficult to establish a U.S. presence and distribution system, for example, and will probably need to enter into alliances, rather than establishing a new product from the ground up in an extremely competitive market.

At their best, alliances capitalise on the strengths of large, multinational corporations while drawing on the benefits that tend to accrue to smaller, more differentiated companies. Creating an integrated organisation from such alliances presents a challenge, however. The overriding issue operationally is how best to maintain a firm, fixed center while encouraging flexibility and proactive approaches to local conditions. Also at issue is the choice of partner. Here, a shared operational philosophy and product/customer orientation are mandatory if the combined whole is to become bigger and more successful than the sum of the parts.

## Capital Markets

As hospitality companies grow into the global economy, they will need to look to global capital markets for support. Investment capital, however, continues to be in short supply and this situation will continue for some time. Companies that wish to attract investors will need to demonstrate that they can offer better returns and performance than in the past. And, at least in the eyes of the world's financial markets, they will need to demonstrate their viability as companies in a global marketplace.

For the first time real estate is now being traded as a commodity in securities markets, and we can therefore expect hospitality products in the future to be viewed in the same manner. The securitisation of real estate in the United States represents a significant trend, and it behooves savvy futurists to track these trends as they develop elsewhere in the world.

Indeed, the world's financial markets are at the cutting edge of globalisation, driven by the revolution in communications. With investment portfolios passed between the Americas, Europe and Asia/Pacific in a time continuum without interruption, 24-hour financial markets are here and are destined to impact significantly the way their customers use them. Hospitality companies that seek capital from the public marketplace will need to function as global enterprises. If the public markets on a global basis are going to serve corporations and produce optimum results, those public companies that feed into any or all of the three major financial centers of the world need to view themselves and to be viewed as global enterprises in order to benefit fully from what these markets have to offer.

Hospitality companies that want to trade in the financial markets will need a business concept that is relatively easy to communicate and comprehend. Those companies that provide homogeneity in products and market orientations will be the most attractive to global capital markets. Companies with simple and well-defined products such as Coca Cola have become recognised by customers and investors around the world. Hospitality companies that want to trade in the financial markets will need a business concept that is relatively easy to communicate and comprehend. A truly global enterprise will have the ability to react quickly to market opportunities, no matter where they present themselves by applying business concepts that have been proven in the context of a global undertaking.

Hotel companies expanding globally will also need to confront varying traditions, structures and attitudes to property investment and valuation in different countries. It is possible that there will be a more common set of standards in the future but we are still far from that level of standardisation.

## Post-Merger Integration in Hospitality

Post-merger integration is one area of particular importance in ensuring that the synergies promised by the deal-makers are in fact delivered after the closing.

There is some evidence to suggest, however, that the benefits of merging companies can be quite elusive. One recent study of post-merger results suggested that approximately one-half of merged entities under-performed their industry rivals following the merger.

*Strategies for Success*

— Drive the merger using a well-articulated overall strategy.

— Choose a partner that fits well rather than one that happens to be available.

— Choose a partner that is similar to you.

— Choose a partner of a different size -same-size mergers can lead to leadership conflict.

— Complete marketing due diligence to discover the opportunities and threats.

— Prioritise key merger initiatives.

— Provide visible leadership from top management.

— Ensure that the transition follows a structured and phased approach.

— Ensure that goals are clearly defined and progress is tracked.

— Manage change from the outset.

— Use best practices to drive the creation of the new organisation and its business processes.

— Use cross-functional teams organised to drive the merger.

— Ensure that communication is well planned and coordinated.

— Recognise that a merger is fraught with risk - avoid taking too much for granted.

— Focus on adding value to the enterprise, while avoiding those actions that can destroy it.

— Avoid the compromises that result from playing to politics.

— Concentrate on key employee retention - some folks may not have the same roles as before, but their value should be recognised and their egos nurtured.

— Identify the leadership who will make the merger work it's a very tough process and not always suitable for managers who have proven to be best at organic growth.

— Don't leave culture clashes left unchecked - culture can be pervasive and the differences in two merged companies can undermine the best laid plans for collaboration.

— The "cultural migration" to the desired organisational behavior is best achieved by visible example along with continuous reinforcement.

— IT systems are frequently incompatible - it's best to come to grips with this reality sooner rather than later.

— Recognise the importance of the company's intangible assets -customers and its own people. Mergers offer great opportunity for competitors to raid the company for its best people and customers.

— Focus on the 80/20 rule and avoid the minutiae - over-analysing to make things perfect is generally ineffective and the delays it causes encourages resistance to change which undermines the plans when they eventually are implemented.

— And finally, don't miss the revenue enhancement opportunities through cross-selling and the development of new products and services for the expanded customer base.

For those already in post-merger mode, it will be too late to deal with the pre-merger issues outlined above. But for the here-and-now, there are clearly a number of post-merger challenges that require a great deal of attention. Those operators who take the time to deal with them proactively will probably be able to mitigate any mistakes made in the pre-merger deal-making phase. They might then be able to move on to ensure that their new and improved company succeeds in beating the challenging odds on post-merger integration success.

## Globalisation of Hospitality Companies

The international expansion has become a necessity for hospitality companies because of the new economic reforms. Hotel companies that do make the decision to go global, as well as those already operating offshore, will benefit from addressing a key area of business risk-physical security and other life safety risks arising from various forms of workplace violence and other crime.

International expansion mergers, deregulation and privatisation often drive revenue growth, operational efficiencies and benefits to customers. But they can also be breeders of employee discontent, labour unrest, potential criminal disruption and terrorist actions. Because of these risks, hospitality organisations doing business in foreign markets should avoid the mistake of replicating the management models, construction design, security systems and training programs that work for them in their home countries.

Just as risk must be carefully assessed in the marketing and financial arenas, hospitality companies also need rigorous risk "audits" when it comes to life safety systems and crisis management. We begin by looking at regional totals in emerging markets for a collection of events that included bombings, hijackings, strikes / protests and sabotage.

*Bombings*

Most prevalent in all regions. In Africa, for example, there were 182 bombings or attempted bombings between 1990 and 1998, while Asia reportings showed a count of 358. Latin America at 344 and the Middle East at 119. Bombings typically result in extensive property damage, high incidence of injury and lengthy disruption of operations, not only to the target company, but to adjoining businesses extending blocks or miles from the bombing target. In March of last year, for example, Colombian authorities were able to foil a plot by guerrillas to detonate a car bomb at a hotel in Colombia.

The hotel was the site of a major international banking conference, with guest speakers including the presidents of Colombia, Panama and Peru. The apparent motive was to show solidarity with guerrilla groups in Peru. In April 1998, an international chain hotel, located in Uganda, was the target of a bombing resulting in five deaths. President Clinton had stayed in this hotel just four days before on his visit to Africa. Since January, Athens, the capital of Greece, has experienced over 150 bombings, directed at diplomatic facilities and foreign business establishments by a terrorist group trying to discourage foreigners from working or operating in Greece.

During October 1997, terrorists attempted to place a truck bomb at a five-star hotel in Colombo, Sri Lanka, but were stopped by hotel security from gaining entrance into the parking lot. The terrorist thereafter parked the vehicle near two other five-star hotels, detonating the device causing major damage to the hotels and surrounding buildings and killing eleven people and wounding 105. The hotels were located near government buildings.

### *Assaults*

The second most frequent offenses reported after bombings. Not included on the earlier table because of the difficulty of capturing total data, assaults take the form of shootings, murder and physical assaults on a person. Various police jurisdictions report high numbers. According to Sao Paulo, Brazil police records, for example. 4,778 people were murdered in Sao Paulo in 1997, averaging 13 homicides per day.

The Brazilian Ministry of Justice reported that 31 of every 100,000 Brazilians are murdered compared to 20 per 100,000 in Mexico and 10 per 100,000 in the United States. The records of the Colombian National Police reflected 31,808 murders or 87 per day in 1997, as well as 204 muggings or assaults committed in Colombia every 24 hours. Mexico City reports more than 250,000 crimes annually or approximately 700 per day.

### *Kidnappings*

This threat has emerged as a problem worldwide, reaching critical levels in Colombia and Mexico. Kidnappings are conducted by terrorists, criminals and others acting for political reasons. Most of the kidnappings are motivated by economic reasons, but in some cases are undertaken to effect political change in a country. Most are resolved peacefully, but some have tragic results.

### *Organised Crime*

The threat from organised crime elements has reached

global proportions. The threat ranges from the well-developed economies of the United States to such places as Hungary, Russia, India, South Africa and other emerging markets. Organised crime groups, sometimes working in concert with distant organisations, are generally engaged in transporting stolen goods internationally, extortion, murder, bombings, drug trafficking, arson and bribery of government officials.

*Corruption*

The International Monetary Fund, World Bank and Inter-American Development Bank are all addressing the issue as it relates to projects with which they are involved. The U.S. Commerce Department estimates that companies worldwide operating outside their own national borders, paid approximately $80 billion in illegal payments or bribes to officials in other countries since 1995. For an industry involved in operating buildings, the fact that corruption is extensive in the construction area should be of particular concern to hospitality managers. Where building inspectors are paid to overlook poorly constructed buildings or lack of compliance with building codes, there is a potential for disaster. Such activity has resulted in a number of incidents, including building collapses resulting in injury and death.

Clearly there are risks for hospitality companies "going global," particularly in markets where there is a history of political and economic instability. Hotel organisations frequently rely on security systems that are transplanted from property to property. But hospitality managers should consider a number of pertinent questions.

- When was the last complete security survey completed for all facilities?

— Is the system sufficient to the threats in the local area?
— Have new risks developed since the last surrey?
— Is there an effective emergency management plan in place?
— Will staff be proficient in its execution?

When reviewing threats in a country or region, it is important to focus not only on what directly appears to affect the hospitality industry, but also on the environment as a totality. A detailed security audit, combined with well-designed life-safety systems and training programs at individual properties, is essential. The following list might be regarded as a minimal risk assessment before venturing into many, if not most, markets outside one's home base of operations. Portions of the checklist also apply to undertaking security audits for hospitality properties planned or in operation in the home country:

### *Threat Assessment*

Prior to physically launching operations, an analysis should be conducted of the country and of the market within which the hotel is located - whether it be a city or non - urban environment. In this process, current threats may be addressed in the immediate market area, as well as in the national context. As appropriate, such a review might also encompass adjacent communities and countries. The risk assessment should encompass the identification of particular criminal problems and crime statistics, as well as the evaluation of local and regional law enforcement agencies. The agency review should in particular focus on an assessment of proficiency, training, degree of professionalism and level of response to incidents.

Once the in-country and market area assessments are complete, the next step is a physical security survey. If done thoroughly at the outset, it may reduce the frequency of need for future assessments. Terrorism, for example, is currently a dominant concern in some environments, but the emphasis can shift quickly if the subject property becomes the target of guest room theft or assaults.

The common link here, however, is perimeter security and access control. Both of these issues should be addressed in the physical security survey. Such a review would not only consider the physical issues such as perimeter security and access control, but also the likely origins of the threat whether it be terrorist, criminal or labour related. The survey should include the identification of vulnerabilities and critical operational components, such as communications, power supply and valuable storage and data processing areas. Furthermore, it should encompass assessment of access control points, perimeter security, alarms/CCTV, lighting and finally a detailed review of security procedures.

New construction should include a crime-prevention design audit. Design for crime prevention in hotel development can he highly beneficial. To be considered are such factors as the relationship of buildings to parking areas and structures, lighting, perimeter views and protection, and security systems.

All hotel employees should have a thorough background check conducted. There have been a number of instances in which hotels have hired individuals with criminal records in illegal drug sales or theft. Incidents of drug dealing. time-clock tampering and guest theft are relatively common problems that can be greatly mitigated with thorough employment and criminal checks. This process is especially important when selecting security personnel. These programs should be developed to enhance security among all hotel staff. in addition to the security force. Employee training should not only include a focus on hotel functions As is the case at most hotels, the security staff is limited and is sometimes strained due to commitments and shrinking staff. By providing the entire hotel staff with training in the identification of security issues, a description of operational methods, where to report information and periodic updates on security advisories management can in effect add additional "eyes" and ears to the organisation.

### *Security Planning*

It is important to broaden the focus of risk and systematise processes. Each hotel, for example should have a detailed bomb threat plan that covers procedures to include: 1) the reporting person; 2) execution of the search plan; 3) what to do if a suspect package is found; and 4) evacuation plans. The process is critical because time is always of the essence. Many bomb threats are made for the purpose of disrupting a company's operations. Needless evacuation of a facility can play into the hands of the person making the threat. On the other hand, information must be properly handled because of the scope of the potential damage.

## Front Office Accounting

Some accounting terminologies used frequently in the front office department. An Account is a form on which financial data are accumulated, summarised and brought to its ending balance. Moreover, all accounts shall have two entries referred to as Debit (dr) (or charges) versus Credit (cr) (or payments). The most widely used representation of accounts is the T-Account, which summarises debit entries on the left-hand side and credit entries on the right-hand side.

Hotels operating under the manual system get use of journal forms to account for different front office accounting transactions. As far as front office accounting is concerned, there are two major types of accounts widely used:

— Guest accounts describe all charges and payments of guests who are already registered at the hotel.

— Non-guest (house or city) accounts: describe all charges and payments of non-guests. To illustrate, a potential guest sending a certain deposit to guarantee a reservation is a non-guest. Moreover, charges and payments of guests who checkout with any method of payment other than cash, shall be opened a non-guest account. Lastly, visitors and employees with charge privileges shall be opened non-guest accounts.

*Folios*: A folio is a statement of all transactions (i.e. debits & credits) affecting the balance of a single account. At Checkout, any guest folio should be balanced to 0 through full cash payment, credit card transfer, personal check transfer, special programme transfer, and direct billing transfer.

The correct way of maintaining folios starts with proper posting, which is the process of recording transactions on a folio (i.e. proper folio, proper location and proper amount). Under the manual, semi automated and fully automated systems, folios are called hand-written folios, machine-posted folios, and computer-based electronic folios respectively. Moreover, all folios shall have a unique serial number for internal control and storing purposes. In the front office department, there are four common types of folios used:

— *Guest folios*: accounts assigned to individual persons or guestrooms

— *Master Folios*: accounts assigned to more than one person or guest room; usually reserved for guest groups

— *Non-Guest (or semi-permanent) folios*: accounts assigned to non-guest businesses or agencies with hotel charge purchase privileges

— *Employee Folios*: accounts assigned to employees with charge purchase privileges

Apart from the above mentioned common folios, front office department get use of some other types of folios such as A-type, B-type, C-type, D-type, and E-type folios.

*Vouchers*: Vouchers depict the details of the transaction information gathered at the source of transaction and is, hence, a supporting documents used only for internal control purposes. Below are some of the commonly used vouchers in the hospitality industry:

— Cash vouchers

— Credit card vouchers

— Charge vouchers

— Transfer vouchers

— Paid-out vouchers

— Correction vouchers

— Allowance vouchers

*Points of sale [POS]*: A point of sale is the location at which goods or services are purchased; sometimes called a revenue center. Moreover, due to technology breakthrough, some non-traditional point of sales emerged such as in-room movie and in-room vending service systems. Since charges are usually incurred at remote points of sale, and guest and non-guest folios are maintained at the front office department, posting of different guest and non-guest charges shall be performed.

An electronic transfer ensures this, under the fully automated system. Under manual and semi automated systems posting shall be done by a physical submission of different vouchers to the front office department.

When posting charges, the following items shall be considered:

— Amount of the charge

— Name of the point of sales outlet

— Room number & name of the guest

— Brief description of the charge

— Guest signature & employee identification

*Ledgers*: The front office ledger is the collection of front office account folios, which usually include guest ledgers (i.e. charges and payments of all guests staying at the hotel). At any moment in time, the account receivable includes the addition of guest ledger and non-guest ledger (or city ledger) which refers to charges and payments of all non-guests.

### *Creation of Guest Accounts*

All guest folios shall be created during the pre-arrival or arrival stage of the guest cycle. Moreover, folios might be either placed in front desk folio tray [i.e. posting tray, folio well, or bucket] or stored as an electronic guest folios in fully automated systems. As far as walk-ins are concerned, all their guest folios are created at the arrival stage!

*Record keeping systems*:

— *Non- automated systems*: Ensured through a series of columns listing individual debit and credit entries accumulated during the occupancy stage after which and establishment of an ending outstanding balance is needed.

— *Semi-automated systems*: Under this very system, all guest transactions should be printed sequentially on a machine-posted folio. Later, the front office clerk needs to come up with the folio outstanding balance. It is extremely important here to mention that, under this very system, each account's previous balance shall be re-entered each time a transaction is posted to the folio.

— *Fully-automated systems*: All guest charges are automatically posted to an electronic folio

*Guest charge privileges*: Potential guests who would like to have guest charge privileges shall present an imprint of an acceptable credit card or direct billing authorisation at registration. Failing to do so, guests would have to pay, in full, all their charges through cash, hence called Paid-in-Advance [PIA] guests and have, hence, have no post status.

*Credit monitoring*: In order to monitor and control charge privileges, the front office clerk should check whether the total net purchases are less than the minimum of floor Limit (i.e.: credit card company's limit) and house limit (i.e. hotel's limit). At least, each day, lists of guests with high risk or high balance accounts shall be communicated to all point of sale outlets. This is vital since, failing to do so, will let point of sales outlets continue giving charge privileges to a point that eventually the credit card company refuses to pay the amount of money exceeding its limit. This will cause very serious financial losses to the hotel.

*Account maintenance*: Whatsoever system hotels operate, maintenance of guest and non-guest accounts is ensured by the following formula:

Net outstanding balance = Previous balance + Debits — Credits

NOB = PB + DR — CR

### *Tracking Transactional Information*

Under the manual and semi-automated systems, tracking transactions is ensured through an intensive use of vouchers. On the other hand, Under fully automated systems, tracking transactions is ensured through on-line electronic transfer of transactional information from remote points of sale to the front office main frame terminal. In accounting, a transaction is an exchange of goods and services for cash or a promise to pay. Under this very assumption, "nothing happens until a transaction occurs". This means that front office clerks shall first of all have a transaction, its supporting documents to be able later to debit or credit certain accounts. In hotels transactions might have the form of:

— *Cash payment*: In this very transaction, front office clerks shall post cash payment as a credit in the guest folio. Moreover, cash vouchers shall be used as a transaction-supporting document.

— *Charge purchase*: Charge purchases represent deferred payment transactions that increase the outstanding balance of a folio account. In this transaction type, front office clerks shall use charge vouchers as a transaction-supporting document.

— *Account correction*: Account correction is used to resolve a posting error in a folio detected at the day the error is made (i.e. before the closing of the business day). In this transaction, front office clerks shall use correction vouchers as a transaction-supporting document.

— *Account allowance*: Account allowances occur because of two reasons:

  — Either as compensation of poor service, or as rebates for coupon discounts. That way, guest outstanding balance decreases.

— As to correct a posting error detected after the closing of the business day.

For both reasons, front office clerks shall prepare an allowance voucher as a transaction supporting document.

— Current transfer

— Cash advance

### *Purpose of Internal Control*

In the hotel industry, the main purpose of internal control is to track transaction documentation, verify account entries and account balances, and to identify vulnerabilities in the accounting system. The keyword to internal control is auditing, which is the process of verifying front office accounting records for accuracy and completeness. Below are some forms that are of extreme importance to internally control, one of the most vital assets in the hotel (i.e. cash):

— *Front office cash sheet*: The front office cash sheet lists each cash receipt or disbursement in order to reconcile cash on hand at the end of a cashier's shift with the documented transaction that occurred during the same shift.

— *Cash, house banks or petty cash*: Petty cash is the amount of cash assigned to a cashier so that he/she can handle the various transactions that occur in a particular work shift. At the beginning of each shift, all cashiers must sign their cash banks and at the end of the shift, shall deposit all cash, checks, and other negotiable instruments in the general cashier's safe deposit box. Moreover, at the end of each shift, cashiers should watch out for cash discrepancies (i.e. any difference between front office cash sheet and the actual amounts in their cash drawers).

Cash discrepancies might have the form of cash overages, shortages, or due backs. Lastly, cashiers might come up with the net cash receipt, which is: Amount of all cash, checks, and other negotiable instruments in cashier's drawer—amount of the initial cash bank + all paid outs

— *Audit control*: Along with the fact that hotels might employ internal control auditors, at least once in a year, (especially for hotels traded in the stock market) to get use of external certified public accountants responsible for approving hotel's accounts.

*Internal control for food*

*Guest Check (also called Server's Checks)*: This initiates the Food & Beverage order taken from the guest, and represents the invoice given to the guest.

— Guest checks should be pre-numbered, tinted and have duplicates. Moreover, it shall be kept in locked storage, in numerical order.
— Used checks, unused checks versus void checks!
— Post to dinner, the server must price and total the guest check (applicable for manual systems), unless the point-of-sale equipment can automatically perform the addition.
— Later, the cashier receives payment or makes the guest sign his/her guest check and deposits everything to the cashier.
— At the end of the shift, the cashier's cash drawer and supporting documents are accounted for (i.e. cash, credit card vouchers, food charges, and any miscellaneous paid-outs). Later, they are reconciled against cash register reading using a daily cashier's report.

— Beverage sales in a lounge, a bar presents a harder job for internal control

— Some basic internal control procedures for beverage sales are listed as follows:

  — Require the bartender to ring each sale as it is made

  — Require the bartender to insert each paid check into a locked box

  — The cash register drawer shall never remain open even for a small period of time

  — Servers are not allowed to first pay the bartender in cash and collect later from customers

  — Bartenders should not be allowed to take register readings or reconcile their own cash at the end of their shifts

Guest charge privileges are allocated to guests who have provided an imprint of a valid credit card or were given a direct billing privilege at registration. In this case, all guest charges are recorded as debits in their respective guest, or master folios.

*Accounts Settlement*

One of the responsibilities of front office clerks is to settle guest accounts, which means the eventual collection of payment for outstanding account balances (i.e. bringing account balances to 0). This is usually ensured either by full cash payment, transfer to an approved credit card, personal check, special programme, or direct billing account. Checkout and settlement describe the activities associated with the final stage of the guest cycle (i.e. departure).

The major activities, which are conducted at departure, include:

— Resolving outstanding guest account balances
— Updating room status information
— Creating guest history records

*Departure Procedures*: At checkout, front office clerks shall:

— Check for mails, messages, and faxes
— Check for safe deposit box, or in-room safe keys
— Post all outstanding charges
— Verify account information
— Inquire about additional recent charges
— Present the guest folio for guest signature
— Verify the method of payment
— Process the account payment (i.e. zeroing out the account)
— Update the room status

*Settlement methods*

— *Full cash payment*: the front office clerk shall destroy the guest's credit card voucher
— *Personal check payment*: the front office clerk shall shift the credit from guest ledger to personal check account, which is a sub-account of the city ledger and the guest shall only sign a personal check voucher
— *Credit card payment*: the front office clerk shall shift the credit from guest ledger to credit card account, which is a sub-account of the city ledger and the guest shall only sign a credit card voucher
— *Special programme payment*: the front office clerk shall shift the credit from guest ledger to special programme account, which is a sub-account of the city ledger and the guest shall only sign a special programme voucher

— *Direct billing payment*: the guest shall sign only his/her folio, and depart. Later, he/she, upon receipt of hotel invoice, shall deposit a certain amount of money in the hotel bank account.

— *Combined settlement method*: In this case, depending on which combination, front office clerk shall proceed by preparing different kinds of vouchers!

*Sales minded cashiers*: As guests tends to depart from the hotel, the cashiers shall approach them in the following way:

— Provide them comment cards and encourage them to use these very cards

— Thank the guest for choosing the hotel and wish him/her a safe trip

— Ask the guest whether he/she is considering returning to the property on any return trip to the area. Cashiers might sometimes accept future reservations!

*Late check out*: Late check out refers to the situation where guests check out after the hotel's established check out time. Late check out shall not be considered as a guest right, rather a privilege which might be honoured by the front office manager upon room availability whether free of charge or charged a late check out fee. There are a lot of innovative ways to check out apart from the traditional way. Below are two commonly used check out options (apply usually only to guests who have provided valid credit cards at registration):

— *Express check out*: This is usually convenient for guests who decide to check out very early in the morning. In fact, at night, bellboys (for example) shall slip the guest folio under the expected departed guestroom. When the guest wakes up, he/she shall sign the gust folio, and the credit card voucher, leave the room, give back the room key to the bellboy, and departs.

- *Self check out*: Guests might check out using self check out terminals situated at public areas or in their rooms if in-room check out systems are integrated with front office main frame.

*Unpaid Account Balances*: Unpaid account balances occur because of the following reasons, most of which are because hotels do not operate fully-automated systems:

- A departing guest honestly forgetting to settle his/her account
- Late charges (being one of the most important reasons)
- Skippers

In order to minimise late charges, front office clerks shall:

- Post transactional vouchers as soon as they arrive at the front desk
- Survey front office equipment, voucher and folio racks for non-posted charges before the front office clerk checks a guest out
- Ask departing guests whether they have incurred any charge purchase or placed long distance telephone calls, which do not appear on their final folio

### *Front Office Records*

The major two front office records that are stored at departure are guest history records (which are stored alphabetically) and guest folios (stored numerically)

#### *Guest history records*

Guest history records are collections of personal & financial data about guests who have stayed at the hotel. Maintaining guest history records helps the hotel better understand its clientele and determine guest trends when they develop. Moreover, these very records might serve as a source of mailing list or to identify guest characteristics that are important to strategic marketing. In addition, they serve as to develop and place advertisements that appeal to the types of clientele the hotel attempts to attract. Finally guest history records points out the need for a new, supplementary, or enhanced services.

Moreover, even though guest history records are stored in the front office department, they are handed to marketing department, whenever needed. In fact, marketing department might get use of guest history records as to create a programme to reward frequent guests with a free stay after a certain number of visits, or as an indicator to watch out for future repeat guest reservations in order to increase the hotel's repeat business market share. Guests tend to remember the friendliness, convenience, and special services that distinguish one property from another. This is called competitive advantage.

### *Functions of Night Audit*

The major functions of the night audit is to:

- Verify posted entries to guest and non-guest accounts
- Balance all front office accounts
- Resolve room status and rate discrepancies
- Monitor guest credit limits
- Produce operational and managerial reports

The night audit requires attention to accounting detail, procedural controls, and guest credit restrictions. In this sense, the night auditor shall track room revenues, occupancy percentages, and other standard operating statistics. He/she shall, also, prepare a daily summary of cash, check, and credit card activities that occurred in the front office department on a daily basis. In night auditing, end of the business day is a vital time for the auditor. As far as the closing of business day is concerned, management shall determine the end of day, which is the time after which the night audit can prepare his/her daily Reports. This end of day is usually the time where the majority of outlets close or no more have frequent activity.

The night auditor shall always compare the data conveyed in different folios against points of sales outlets daily reports, housekeeping room status report. This is called cross-referencing, and is a vital procedure in the internal control. After comparing, the night auditor should come up with the guest, non-guest, and departmental accounts. This total should match the daily POS totals (i.e. in balance). If not, then the auditor is said to be out-of-balance, and the night auditor shall substantially review all account statements, vouchers, support documents, and departmental source of documentation in order to bring the audit to balance.

The night audit shall compare all credit limits of guests and non-guests accounts with credit card floor limits, hotel's house limit, guest's status and reputation. If high balance accounts are detected, the night auditor shall note and report this to management the following day. Under the manual, a daily transcript and a supplementary transcript are used to track daily transactions of guest and non-guest accounts respectively. Hotels operating under semi-automated systems use D-Cards for the same purpose.

*Non-automated system*: under this very system, 4 forms are widely used, which are:

— Daily and supplementary transcripts

— Guest and non-Guest folios

— Front office cash sheets

*Semi-automated system*: The audit of guest and non-guest accounts is ensured mostly through mechanical or electronic posting machines. The most important form obtained under this very system is the D Card.

*Fully-automated system*: This very system is the best compared to manual and semi-automated systems. In fact, this system can be interfaced with point of sale terminals, call accounting systems, and other revenue centers for quick, accurate and automatic postings to electronic guest and non-guest account folios. This very fact enables the night auditor to concentrate more on auditing transactions and analysing front office activities.

*Night Audit Process*: The night audit process focuses on two areas:

— Discovery and correction of front office accounting errors ensured through the cross-referencing process.

— Creation of accounting and managerial reports including audit balance, average rate, occupancy percentage, usage of package plans and other marketing programmes, and the number of group rooms and complementary rooms occupied.

The main steps of the night audit process are:

— Complete outstanding posting

— Reconcile room status discrepancies

— Verify room rates

— Balance all departmental accounts

— Verify no-show reservations

— Post room rates and taxes

— Prepare required reports

— Prepare cash receipts for deposit

— Clear or back up the system

— Distribute reports

Most of the errors encountered in the night audit process stem from the fact that the hotel is not operating under fully automated system. The widely occurring errors in the night audit process can have the form of:

— Pickup errors

— Transposition errors

— Missing folios

# 2

# Basics of Financial Accounting

The accounting system provides the financial information needed to evaluate the effectiveness of current and past operations. In the past, much of the work required to maintain an effective accounting system involved extensive manual effort that was tedious, aggravating, and time consuming. Such systems relied on individual effort to continually record transactions, to add, subtract, summarise, and check for errors.

The rapid advancement of computer technology has increased operating speed, data storage, and reliability, accompanied by a significant cost reduction. Inexpensive microcomputers and accounting software programmes have advanced to the point where all of the posting, calculations, error checking, and financial reports are provided quickly by the computerised system.

The efficiency and cost-effectiveness of accounting computer software allow management to maintain direct personal control of the accounting system. Financial accounting is concerned with the recording of financial transactions and analysing the effect of such transactions to assist in the development of business decisions. In addition, financial accounting provides information in the form of balance sheets, income statements, and other financial statements to users outside of businesses that are in some way concerned or affected by the performance of the business-stockholders, creditors, lenders, governmental agencies, and other outside users.

Hospitality management accounting is concerned with providing specialised internal information to managers who are responsible for directing and controlling operations within the hospitality industry. Internal information is the basis for planning alternative short- or long-term courses of action and the decision as to which course of action is selected. Specific detail is provided as to how the selected course of action will be implemented.

Managers direct the needed material resources and motivate the human resources needed to carry out a selected course of action. Managers control the implemented course of action to ensure that the plan is being followed and, as necessary, modified to meet the objectives of the selected course of action.

## Career Opportunities in Hospitality Accounting

For the student interested in accounting, there are a variety of career opportunities in the hospitality industry. First, there is general accounting, which includes the recording and production of accounting information and/or specialisation in a particular area such as food service and beverage cost control. Second, larger organisations might offer careers in the design (or revision) and implementation of accounting systems.

A larger organisation might also offer careers in budgeting, tax accounting, and auditing that verifies accounting records and reports of individual properties in the chain.

Hospitality business operations, as well as others, are generally identified as having a number of different cyclical sales revenue cycles.

— there is the daily operating cycle that applies particularly to restaurant operations where daily sales revenue typically depends on meal periods.

— there is a weekly cycle. On one hand, business travellers normally use hotels, motels, and other hospitality operations during the week and provide little weekend hospitality business. On the other hand, local people most often frequent restaurants on Friday through Sunday more than they do during the week.

— there is a seasonal cycle that depends on vacationers to provide revenue for hospitality operations during vacation months.

— a generalised business cycle will exist during recessionary inflationary cycles, and hospitality operations typically experience a major decline in sales revenue.

The various repetitive accounting cycles encountered in hospitality operations create unique difficulties in forecasting sales revenue and operating costs. In particular, variable costs (e.g., cost of sales and labour costs) require unique planning procedures that assist in budget forecasting. Since hospitality operations are people-oriented and people-driven, it is more difficult to effectively automate and control hospitality costs than in other nonhospitality business sectors.

Unfortunately, most accounting textbooks and generalised accounting courses emphasize accounting systems using procedures and applications that are applicable to services, retailing, and manufacturing businesses. These types of businesses do not normally require the use of the unique accounting procedures and techniques required by hospitality operations. In manufacturing operations, all costs are generally assigned to products or product lines and identified as direct costs and indirect costs. Direct costs include all materials and labour costs that are traceable directly to the product manufactured.

Indirect costs generally refer to manufacturing or factory overhead, and include such items as administrative salaries, wages and miscellaneous overhead, utilities, interest, taxes, and depreciation. The basic nature of indirect costs presents difficulties isolating specific costs since they are not directly traceable to a particular product. Portions of supporting indirect costs are assigned by allocation techniques to each product or product line.

However, a hospitality operation tends to be highly departmentalised with separate operating divisions that provide rooms, food, beverage, banquet, and gift shop services. A hospitality accounting system must allow an independent evaluation of each operating department and its operating divisions.

Costs directly traceable to a department or division are identified as direct costs. Typically, the major direct costs include cost of sales (cost of goods sold), salary and wage labour, and specific operating supplies. After direct costs are determined, they are deducted from sales revenue to isolate contributory income, which represents the department's or division's contribution to support undistributed indirect costs of the whole operation.

Indirect costs are not easily traceable to a department or division. Generally, no attempt is made at this stage of the evaluation to allocate indirect costs to the department or divisions. Managers review operating results to ensure that contributory income from all departments or divisions is sufficient to cover total indirect costs for the overall hospitality operation and provide excess funds to meet the desired level of profit.

## General Financial Accounting Systems

Managerial analysis is enhanced with an understanding of the information provided by an accounting system. Without management's understanding of the information being provided, management effectiveness will be greatly reduced.

Financial accounting is a common language developed by accountants over time to define the principles, concepts, procedures, and broad rules necessary for management's use in a viable accounting system for making decisions and maintaining an efficient, effective, and profitable business. An account is a record in which the current status of each type of asset, liability, owners' equity, sales revenue, and expense is kept.

The balance is the current status of an account-the amount that is in a particular account at a specific point in time. An accounting system shows detailed information regarding each of the account categories, and it governs recording, reporting, and preparation of financial statements that show the financial condition of a business entity. The accounting period is the time period covered by the financial statements.

### *Cash and Accrual Accounting*

The cash and accrual basis are the two methods of accounting. The difference between the two methods is how and when sales revenue and expenses are recognised. The cash basis of accounting recognises sales revenue inflows when cash is received and operating expense outflows to generate sales revenue when cash is paid. Simply put, the cash basis recognises sales revenue and operating expenses only when cash changes hands. The accrual basis of accounting recognises inflows of sales revenue when earned and operating expense outflows to produce sales revenues when incurred; it does not matter when cash is received or paid. Many small operations use the cash basis of accounting for their type of business; no requirement exists to prepare and report their financial position to external users.

The cash basis can be computed as follows:

Beginning cash + Cash sales revenue - Cash payments = Ending cash

There is no basic equation for the accrual basis.

To illustrate cash accounting, assume that a new restaurant purchased and sold inventory on a cash basis for two months of operation. A partial income statement prepared on a cash basis for the first two months of operation, assuming monthly sales revenue of $10,000 and total inventories of $8,000 for resale, would show the following:

| | Month 1 | Month 2 |
|---|---|---|
| Cash sales revenue | $10,000 | $10,000 |
| Cash purchases | ( 8,000) | -0- |
| Gross margin (before other expenses) | $ 2,000 | $10,000 |

This method gives a distorted view of the operations over the two months. The combined two-month gross margin (or gross profit) would be $12,000; however, the accrual method will give a more accurate picture of the real situation, a gross margin (before other expenses) of $6,000 each month. In the following accrual example, cost of sales is estimated at 40% of sales revenue. Cost of sales refers to cost of goods sold.

| | Month 1 | Month 2 |
|---|---|---|
| Cash sales revenue | $10,000 | $10,000 |
| Cash purchases | ( 4,000) | ( 4,000) |
| Gross margin (before other expenses) | $ 6,000 | $ 6,000 |

The examples given are not meant to suggest that the cash basis of accounting is never used. Many small businesses find the cash basis appropriate. However, the cash basis is not considered adequate for medium and larger business organisations, which normally use the accrual basis of accounting.

The accrual method is used throughout this text, except in cases where cash management supplements the decision-making process. Without a basic knowledge of the accounting system and the information provided, it will be difficult to produce or understand financial reports. The two major financial reports are the balance sheet and income statement.

### *Balance Sheet*

The balance sheet reveals the financial condition of a business entity by showing the status of its assets, liabilities, and ownership equities on the specific ending date of an operating period. The income statement reports the economic results of the business entity by matching sales revenue inflows, and expense outflows to show the results of operations-net income or net loss. The income statement is generally considered the more important of the two major financial reports. Since it reports the results of operations, it clearly identifies sales revenue inflows and the cost outflows to produce sales revenue.

The balance sheet provides an easier basis for understanding double-entry accounting. The accounting equation, as it is known, consists of three key elements and defines the basic format of the balance sheet.

The balance sheet equation is A = L + OE.

— *Assets (A):* Resources of value used by a business entity to create sales revenue, which, in turn, increases assets.

— *Liabilities (L):* Debt obligations owed to creditors as a result of operations to generate sales revenue; to be paid in the near future with assets. Liabilities represent creditor equity or claims against the assets of the business entity.

— *Ownership equity (OE):* Ownership equity represents claims to assets of a business entity.

There are three basic forms of ownership equity:

— Proprietorship-entity financing provided by a sole owner.

— Partnership-entity financing provided by two or more owners (partners).

— Corporation-a legal entity incorporated under the laws of a state, separate from its owners.

*Capital stock:* Financing provided by stockholders (or shareholders) with ownership represented by shares of corporate stock. Each share of stock represents one ownership claim.

*Retained earnings:* Earnings of the corporation that have been kept in the business after dividends are paid.

The equality point indicates an absolute necessity to maintain the same on both sides of the equation. The sum total of the left side of the equation, total assets, A, must equal the total sum of the right side of the equation, liabilities, L, plus ownership equity, OE. When a transaction affects both sides of the equation, equality of the equation must be maintained. One side of the equation cannot increase or decrease without the other side increasing or decreasing by the same amount. If a transaction occurs that affects only one side of the equation, total increases must equal total decreases.

The assets consumed produce sales revenue that become cost of sales and operating expenses. The liabilities and ownership equity elements of the equation represent the claims against assets by creditors (liabilities) and claims against the assets by the ownership (OE).

### *Double-Entry Accrual Accounting*

The analysis of accounting transactions, the recording, posting, adjusting, and reporting economic results and financial condition of a business entity is the heart of double-entry accrual accounting. For an accounting transaction to occur, at least one element of the balance sheet equation or the income statement elements must be created or changed. An exchange between a business entity where services are rendered or goods are sold to an external entity for cash or on credit, or where services are received or goods are purchased creates a transaction. Following the transaction, adjusting entries must be made to adjust the operating accounts of the business entity at the end of an operating period to recognise internal accruals and deferrals.

Such transactions will recognise sales revenues earned but not yet received or recorded, and expenses incurred but not yet paid or recorded. To complete the accounting period, a requirement also exists to close the temporary income statement operating accounts (sales revenue and expenses) to bring them to a zero balance and transfer net income or net loss to the capital account(s) or the retained earnings account. Note that this requirement means that an entry is made on both sides of the equation-thus, the name double-entry accounting.

Since no transaction can affect only one account, the balance sheet equation is kept in balance and the equality between both sides of the equation, A = L + OE, is maintained. Each transaction directs the change to be made to each account involved in the transaction. Each directed change will cause an increase or decrease in the stated dollar amount to a specified account. It is important to understand how a journal entry directs such changes to a specific account. This is accomplished through the use of two account columns to receive numerical values that follow the rules of debit and credit entries.

## Generally Accepted Accounting Principles (GAAP)

Accounting is not a static system; it is a dynamic process that incorporates generally accepted accounting principles (GAAP) that evolve to suit the needs of financial statement readers, such as business managers, equity owners, creditors, and governmental agencies with meaningful, dependable information.

### *Business Entity Operating Principles*

From an accounting, if not from a legal, point of view, the transactions of a business entity operating as a proprietorship, partnership, or corporation are considered to be separate and distinct from all personal transactions of its owners. The separation of personal transactions of the owners from the business entity must be maintained, even if the owners work in or for the business entity.

Only changes to assets, liabilities, ownership equity, and other transactions of the business entity are entered to the organisation's accounting records. The ownership's personal assets, debts, and expenses are not part of the business entity.

### *Monetary Unit Principle*

The assumption of the monetary unit principle is that the primary national monetary unit is used for recording numerical values of business exchanges and operating transactions. The U.S. monetary unit is the dollar. Thus, the accounting function in the case records the dollar value of sales revenue inflows and expense outflows of the business entity during its operations. The monetary unit of the dollar also expresses financial information within the financial statements and reports. Information provided and maintained in the accounting system is recorded in dollars.

### *Going Concern Principle*

Under normal circumstances, the going concern principle makes the assumption that a business entity will remain in operation indefinitely. This continuity of existence assumes that the cost of business assets will be recovered over time by way of profits that are generated by successful operations. The balance sheet values for long-lived assets such as land, building, and equipment are shown at their actual acquisition cost. Since there is no intention to sell such assets, there is no reason to value them at market value. The original cost of a long-lived physical asset (other than land) is recovered over its useful life using depreciation expense.

### *Principle of Cost*

The assumption made by the monetary concept is tied directly to the cost principle, which requires the value of business transactions be recorded at the actual or equivalent cash cost. During extended periods of inflation or deflation, comparing income statements for different years becomes difficult, if not meaningless, under the stable dollar assumption. However, some exceptions are made with the valuation of inventories for resale, and also to express certain balance sheet and income statement items in terms of current, rather than historic dollars.

### *Time Period Principle*

The time period principle requires a business entity to complete an analysis to report financial condition and profitability of its business operation over a specific operating time period. An ongoing business operates continuously. For example, electrical power in reality flows continuously to the user, yet in theory the flow stops when the service meter reading is recorded.

The billing statement says that service for the period technically ended at a certain date, although service continued without interruption. This example relates to a monthly period; however, the theory applies to any time period-daily, weekly, monthly, quarterly, semiannually, or annually. An accounting year is an accounting period of one year. A fiscal year is for any 12 consecutive months and does not necessarily coincide with a calendar year that begins on January 1 and ends on December 31 of the same year. In the hospitality business, statements are frequently prepared on a monthly and, in some cases, a weekly basis.

### *Principles of Conservatism*

A business should never prepare financial statements that will cause balance sheet items such as assets to be overstated or liabilities to be understated, sales revenues to be overstated, or expenses to be understated. Situations might exist where estimates are necessary to determine the inventory values or to decide an appropriate depreciation rate. The inventory valuation should be lower rather than higher. Conservatism in this situation increases the cost of sales and decreases the gross margin (also called the gross profit).

The costs of long-lived assets (other than land) are systematically recovered through depreciation expense, and should be higher rather than lower. Conservatism in this case will increase expenses and, therefore, lower reported operating income; its goal is to avoid overstating operating income. However, caution must be exercised to ensure that conservatism is not taken to the extreme, creating misleading results. For example, restaurant equipment with an estimated five-year life could be fully depreciated in its first year of use. Although this procedure is certainly conservative, it is hardly realistic.

### *Consistency Principle*

The consistency principle was established to ensure comparability and consistency of the procedures and techniques used in the preparation of financial statements from one accounting period to the next. For example, the cash basis requires that cash be exchanged before sales revenue or expenses can be recognised, while the accrual basis of accounting requires recognition of sales revenue when earned and expenses when incurred. Switching back and forth between the two would not be consistent, nor would a random change in inventory valuation methods from one period to the next.

When changes made are not consistent with the last accounting period, the full disclosure principle, requires informing probable and potential readers of the statements of such changes. The disclosure should show the economic effects of the changes on financial results of the current period and the probable economic impact on future periods.

### *Concept of Materiality*

Theoretically, items that may affect the decision of a user of financial information are considered important or material, and must be reported in a correct way. The materiality concept allows immaterial small dollar amount items to be treated in an expedient although incorrect manner. In the conservatism, an item of restaurant equipment with a five-year life could be fully depreciated in its first year. This technique would be considered overlay conservative, particularly if it has a material effect to operating income.

Consider the alternatives. First, equipment costing $50,000 with no estimated residual value could be fully depreciated the first year to maximize depreciation expense, thus reducing operating income. Second, the equipment could be systematically depreciated over each year of estimated life, to allocate depreciation expense charges against sales revenue in each year of serviceable life.

Depreciating equipment systematically each year over the life of the asset provides the most realistic alternative. This technique recovers the cost of a longlived physical asset by allocating depreciation expense based on the consumption of the benefits received from the asset over five years of use. However, a restaurant might have purchased a supply of letterhead stationery for use over the next five years at a cost of $200. The restaurant could show the total amount of $200 as an expense in the year purchased, opting not to expense the stationery at $40 per year over five years. Operating income would not be materially affected by completely expensing the purchase in year one.

### *Full Disclosure Principle*

Financial statements are primarily concerned with a past period. The full disclosure principle states that any future event that may or will occur, and that will have a material economic impact on the financial position of the business, should be disclosed to probable and potential readers of the statements. Such disclosures are most frequently made by footnotes.

For example, a hotel should report the building of a new wing, or the future acquisition of another property. A restaurant facing a lawsuit from a customer who was injured by tripping over a frayed carpet edge should disclose the contingency of the lawsuit. Similarly, if accounting practices of the current financial statements were changed and differ from those previously reported, the changes should be disclosed. Changes from one period to the next that affect current and future business operations should be reported if possible.

Changes of this nature include changes made to the method used to determine depreciation expense or to the method of inventory valuation; such changes would increase or decrease the value of ending inventory, cost of sales, gross margin, and net income or loss. All changes disclosed should indicate the dollar effects such disclosures have on financial statements.

***Objectivity Principle***

This objectivity principle requires a transaction to have a basis in fact. Some form of objective evidence or documentation must exist to support a transaction before it can be entered into the accounting records. Such evidence is the receipt for the payment of a guest check or the acceptance of a credit card, or the record of billing a house account-account of a hotel guest-that supports earned sales revenue. The accrual basis of accounting recognises sales revenue when earned, not necessarily when received. Sales revenue is earned when cash is received or when credit is given, thereby creating accounts receivable-a record of the amount expected to be received in the near future.

Expenses are incurred when cash is paid or when credit is received, creating an accounts payable on which payment is to be made in the near future. If payment of a receivable becomes uncollectible, it may be written off as bad debt expense (income statement method for income tax purposes). An uncollectible account may also be written off through the creation of an allowance for uncollectable accounts (balance sheet method for financial reporting purposes). The allowance for uncollectible accounts may be established to provide for future bad debts. However, the creation of an allowance account for bad debts (balance sheet method) is an example of an exception to the objectivity concept.

The allowance account has no absolute basis in fact because it relates to future events that might or might not occur. However, the allowance account for bad debts is normally based on past historical experience on the percentage of receivables not collected. Evidence of past receivables that were not collected is considered supporting evidence within the bounds of the objectivity concept and the conservatism concept.

### *Matching Principle*

The matching principle reinforces the accrual basis of accounting. Assets are consumed to generate sales revenue inflows while outflows of assets are identified as operating expenses. The matching principle requires that for each accounting period all sales revenues earned must be recognised, whether payment is received or not. It also requires the recognition of all operating expenses incurred, whether paid or not paid during the period. Sales revenue is recognised when earned and operating expenses are recognised when incurred, regardless of when cash is received or paid.

The matching principle also conforms to the timing of the recognition of sales revenue inflows and expense outflows that allow matching of sales revenue to expenses for an accounting period. When a profit-directed operation ends its operating period, it seeks to determine the best estimate of operating results-net income or net loss. When total sales revenue is greater than total expenses, net income will exist. When total sales revenue is less than total expenses, a net loss will exist. The financial statement that discloses financial results for an accounting period is the income statement. If all sales revenues earned and operating expenses incurred at the end of an operating period are not recognised, the resulting net income or net loss will not provide the most accurate estimate of profit or loss.

If a depreciable asset is disposed of, the total accumulated depreciation charges over its life are deducted from its original cost to find its book value. When a long-lived asset is sold, traded, or otherwise disposed of, the book value of the asset is matched against the value received (not original historical cost) to determine if a gain or loss is to be recognised at its disposal.

## Ledger Account and Debit Functions

In a manual accounting system, the general ledger maintains separate accounts for each type of accounting transaction. These accounts are identified by name and account number using a standardised format. Ledger accounts are necessary to record transactions on all items reported on the financial statements. The ledger account records each dollar value posted and reports the account balance after each entry is posted. The journal entry is the source of instructions that identifies a specific account by name, the dollar value, and the debit or credit column to be entered. The effect of the debit or credit entry will increase or decrease the balance of the account posted, depending on whether the normal balance is a debit- or credit-balanced account.

A modified T account is a simple format used to aid in understanding account posting. This format shows a continuous balance that eliminates the need to total the debit and credit columns to find the correct balance of an account. The same principle of posting dollar amounts to the left or debit column and the right or credit column applies whether a manual or computerised system is being used. A modified T format shows the key elements of a ledger account. The use of this format is more than adequate for academic understanding.

### *Rules of Debit-Credit Functions*

Assets are debit-balanced accounts and are increased by debits and decreased by credits. Liabilities and ownership equity accounts are credit-balanced and increased by credits and decreased by debits. The debit-credit rules as applied to the balance sheet equation are summarised as follows:

Assets = Liabilities + Ownership equity

Sales revenue accounts are credit-balanced accounts; credits increase a creditbalanced account and debits decrease a credit-balanced account. Expense accounts are debit-balanced; debits increase a debit-balanced account and credits decrease a debit-balanced account.

## End of Period Adjusting Entries

Adjusting entries are needed to ensure that information for the income statement and the balance sheet will be as accurate as possible. Generally, an operating period is one year. A calendar year begins on January 1 and ends on December 31 of the same year. In addition to annual periods, many organisations operate on monthly, quarterly, or semiannual operating periods.

At the end of an operating period, adjustments are made to recognise all sales revenue earned. This might be sales revenue not yet recorded or sales revenue that was earned but will not be received until sometime in the new accounting period. Adjustment must also be made to recognise expenses not yet recorded or expenses that were incurred in the current period but not expected to be paid until sometime in the new operating period. Adjusting entries are needed to ensure that correct amounts of sales revenue and expenses are reported in the income statement, and to ensure that the balance sheet reports the proper assets and liabilities. Adjusting entries are also used for items that, by their nature, are normally deferred. These consist of two types of adjustments:

— *The use or consumption of an asset and recognition of it as an expense*: This type of adjustment typically adjusts supplies, prepaid expenses, and depreciable assets.

— *The reduction of a liability and recognition of sales revenue*: This adjustment concerns the recognition of unearned revenue as being recognised as earned.

Operating supplies are assets until they are consumed. At the end of a period, the difference between the balance in the supplies ledger account and the value of supplies remaining in inventory represents the amount consumed that needs to be expensed. Assume that a supplies account had a balance of $1,200 at the end of an operating period and that supplies on hand were $400. Thus, $1,200 - $400 = $800 of supplies were used. The adjusting entry is:

| Account | Debit | Credit |
|---|---|---|
| Supplies expense | $800 | |
| Supplies | | $800 |

All prepaid items such as prepaid rent and prepaid insurance are paid for in advance and are considered to be assets from which benefits will be received over the life of the prepaid. The amount of a prepaid asset to be expensed over its expected life can be expressed in months or years:

Cost of the prepaid / Life (time) = Amount expensed

For example, assume rent was prepaid for the next two years for $24,000. The rent expense for one year would be

$12,000 ($24,000 / 2 years), or $1,000 per month ($24,000 / 24 months):

| Account | Debit | Credit |
|---|---|---|
| Rent expense | $12,000 | |
| Prepaid rent | | $12,000 |

Period-ending monthly adjustments are needed to ensure that financial statements are based on accurate data. The income statement and balance sheet must conform to the principle of matching sales revenues to expenses, and must include those end-of-period adjustments as are necessary to recognise accruals and deferrals.

Accruals represent end-of-period adjustments recognising sales revenue earned and expenses incurred, with the receipt of payment or the making of payment expected to occur in the next accounting period. Deferrals represent endof-period adjustments to revenues and expenses, and also include adjustments to assets and liabilities to reflect sales revenue earned and expenses incurred.

### *Sales and Inventory Adjustment*

Any business purchasing inventory or producing it for resale will not expect to sell all items available during an accounting period. A restaurant operation will always maintain a minimum food and beverage inventory to take care of current daily and near-future business operations. At the end of an accounting period, the cost of inventory sold is identified as an expense described as cost of sales (CS). Ending inventory (EI) not sold will continue to be classified as an asset and is not expensed. Cost of sales (CS) describes cost of goods sold. It is determined easily:

Use the beginning inventory (BI), add inventory purchases (P), and deduct inventory not sold.

Several different methods may be used to adjust the inventory for resale accounts to find cost of inventory sold. Normally, the first of two adjustments requires that cost of sales be debited in the amount equal to the balance of the inventory account, followed by crediting to the inventory account equal to its balance. Posting the entry brings the inventory to a zero balance, and in effect transfers the inventory account balance to the cost of sales account. The next adjustment requires the value of ending inventory to be debited to the inventory account and credited to the cost of sales account, and the second entry restores the inventory account to the value of the end of the period closing inventory.

Posting the adjusting entry will create the cost of sales account, thereby adjusting the food inventory account to the correct ending balance.

### *Adjustments of Prepaid Expenses*

When expenses are paid in advance for future periods, normally exceeding a month, for such items as rent or insurance, a prepaid asset account is created. The prepaid item names the benefit to be received and consumed as an expense over a specified number of time periods (e.g., months, quarters, or years). In the example, Texana Restaurant paid in advance $3,600 for a two-year insurance policy on May 6. If the prepaid is expensed monthly, insurance expense for the month of May will be $150 per month ($3,600 / 24). The prepaid insurance account will be reduced $150 and the insurance expense account will increase by $150 when the journal entry is posted.

Prepaid cost / life of prepaid = Amount expensed per period

Prepaid / months = \$3,600 / 24 = \$150 per month

Alternative: Prepaid cost / years = \$3,600 / 2 = \$1,800 per year, or

\$1,800 per year / 12 months = \$150 per month

The adjusting journal entry to reduce the prepaid insurance account and recognise one month of insurance expense. Posting of the adjusting journal entry creates the insurance expense account and adjusts the prepaid insurance account.

### *Wages and Salaries Accrual Adjustments*

Payday seldom falls on the last day of the month. It is not unusual for wages and salaries to be earned but not paid by the end of the month. An accrual adjusting entry is made to record payroll expense belonging to the month just ended. This adjustment ensures that the income statement and balance sheet reflect the correct expense and payroll payable.

### *Depreciation Expense Adjustments*

Depreciation is the systematic expensing of the cost of a long-lived physical asset (except land) that provides economic benefits in excess of one year. Estimated value recovered at the end of the asset's serviceable life, such as trade in value, salvage, or scrap value, is referred to as residual value. All long-lived depreciable assets must remain in the accounting records at their historical cost. This requirement precludes the reduction of the depreciable asset's cost when depreciation expense is recognised. It necessitates the creation of a special offset account called a contra asset account to depreciation expense. The offset account has the task of recording and accumulating all depreciation expense charges that occur over the life of the depreciable long-lived asset. The account is named to identify its purpose and is called accumulated depreciation. It has a credit balance. Each depreciable asset has a specific creditbalanced, accumulated depreciation account assigned by name and ledger account number.

The balance of the accumulated depreciation account is used to determine the book value of a depreciable asset in the event the asset is disposed of. The book value is used to determine whether a gain or loss has occurred on the disposal of a depreciable asset. If the value received for the depreciable asset is greater than its book value, a gain is recognised. Conversely, if the value received for the asset is less than its book value, a loss is recognised. Each depreciable asset is shown on the balance sheet as a fixed asset and shows its historical cost minus the balance of its accumulated depreciation account as its book value.

*Straight-line depreciation*

Straight-line depreciation breaks depreciation expense to be recovered into equal periods, such as months, quarters, half years, or years. Texana Restaurant purchased equipment and a building on May 5, 2006. Straight-line depreciation systematically breaks the amount to be recovered through depreciation expense into equal amounts over its estimated useful life based on given time periods-months, quarters, and years. Straight line is not accelerated over the early years of a depreciable asset's useful life. Straight-line depreciation will be described using the equipment and building based on monthly and yearly periods. Monthly depreciation is used in the continuing illustration for the Texana Restaurant.

*Equipment Depreciation Calculation:* Purchased equipment for $12,000 that has an 8-year estimated life and no residual value. (Cost - Residual / Life) = Depreciation expense per period:

Cost - Residual / Life = $12,000 / 96 months

= $125 depreciation expense per month

Cost - Residual / Life = $12,000 / 8 years

= $1,500 depreciation expense per year

*Building Depreciation Calculation:* Purchased a building for $150,000 that has a 25-year life and a residual value of $30,000. (Cost - Residual / Life) = Depreciation expense:

(Cost - Residual / Life) = Depreciation expense:

$150,000 - $30,000 / 300 months = $400 per month

(Cost - Residual / Life) = Depreciation expense:

$150,000 - 30,000 / 25 years = $4,800 per year

*Production depreciation method*

Units-of-production depreciation shares some of the elements of straight line depreciation. Cost minus residual remains the numerator, and the denominator again expresses the life of the asset. However, the life of the asset is expressed in units. Miles driven, gallons produced, and hours used are a few examples. Assume that a van was purchased for $29,800 with an estimated residual value of $1,800 based on a life of 140,000 miles. During the month of May, the van recorded 580 miles of use. The depreciation expense is calculated as follows:

(Cost - Residual) / Life in units = Depreciation expense per unit x Units used - Depreciation expense

($29,800 = $1,800) / 140,000 = $28,000 / 140,000 = $0.20 per mile

$0.20 per mile x 580 = $116 Depreciation expense

Subsequent months or years of depreciation would be calculated in the same manner by using the depreciation rate per mile multiplied by the miles driven. In a generic sense, both straight-line and units-of-production methods are based on the consumption of a depreciable asset. Time periods is the basis for straight line depreciation. Units of production uses units as the basis of use or consumption during a time period. The production method estimates the life of the depreciable asset, as does the straight-line method, and is useful for budgeting purposes. Like the straight-line method, units of production provide the ability to create accelerated depreciation expense charges.

### *Sum-of-the-Years'-Digits Depreciation*

Commonly called SYD, sum-of-the-years'-digits depreciation is an accelerated depreciation method that allows greater amounts of depreciation to be expensed in the early years of a depreciable asset's life. An accelerated method presumes that an asset becomes less and less efficient over its life. Thus, it allows the matching of depreciation to the efficiency loss of the asset over time. SYD determines the amount to be depreciated using a fraction multiplied by the cost minus the residual value.

The maximum years of a depreciable asset's life becomes the numerator in the first year and then reduces the numerator by one in each subsequent year of the asset's life. The denominator of the fraction is found by summing the years of an asset's life, or by using an equation. An example using each method of determining the denominator will be based on equipment, which is purchased for $34,200 with a life of five years and a residual value of $600:

Additive function:

Yr 1 + Yr 2 = 3 + Yr 3 = 6 + Yr 4 = 10 + Yr 5 = 15 is the denominator

The additive function can be somewhat cumbersome as the years of life of the depreciable asset increase. Both methods determine the denominator, which represents 100% of the amount to be depreciated. The letter in the equation represents the number of years in a depreciable asset's life:

$$\frac{n(n+1)}{2}=\frac{5(5+1)}{2}=\frac{5\times 6}{2}=\frac{30}{2}=15 \text{ is the denominator}$$

The equation to calculate SYD depreciation for each year of the asset's life is:

SYD fraction x Cost - Residual = Depreciation expense

The numerator of the fraction will begin with the maximum years of the asset's life in the first year, minus one for each subsequent year.

*Double-declining-balance depreciation*

The double-declining-balance method, also called DDB depreciation. This method doubles the straight line depreciation rate (1/Years) to find a DDB%. This method, unlike straight line, units of production, and SYD, ignores any type of residual value in the calculation of the depreciation expense. The DDB% is multiplied by book value to determine the amount of depreciation expense.

In the first year, no accumulated depreciation account exists until after the depreciation expense is calculated, journalised, and posted. Thus, in the first year, the book value of an asset using the DDB method is the depreciable assets' cost - accumulated depreciation, which is cost - zero because no previous depreciation expense was recorded.

After the first year of DDB depreciation expense is posted, the book value changes to cost - first-year depreciation expense. In subsequent years, book value will decrease each year by the amount of depreciation expense charged in the previous year.

Although the DDB method ignores residual values in calculating the yearly depreciation expense, the book value of an asset that is fully depreciated may be greater than, but must not be less than, cost minus residual value if residual value exists. Assume equipment that had a five-year life and a residual value of $1,000 was purchased for $16,000. The DDB equation is stated next, followed by each equation element:

DDB% x Book value = Depreciation expense

— DDB% is calculated as 100%, or 1 divided by years of life:

  100% / 5 = 20% x 2 = 40%, or 1 / 5 = 20% x 2 = 40%

  In other words, the straight-line rate has doubled.

— Alternative: Since DDB% doubles the straight-line rate, the numerator can be expressed as follows:

  100% x 2 = 200%, or 2 divided by years of life = 2 / 5 = 40%

— Book value = Cost - Accumulated depreciation.

— Depreciation expense is DDB% Book x value.

## Closing Journal Entries

The general ledger showing the posted operating and adjusting journal entries is shown for review. The general ledger is the source used to prepare an adjusted trial balance that confirms the ledger accounts are in balance.

Before determining operating income or loss, an adjusted trial balance is prepared by extracting each ledger account by name and balance, after adjustments are posted. The last step in moving through the accounting cycle is to create closing entries, bringing the temporary accounts balances to zero. Closing the temporary accounts will transfer sales revenue and operating expenses to the income summary account. The income summary account receives sales revenue and expenses including cost of sales; its final balance represents operating income or net loss.

Closing the income summary account will transfer operating income or operating loss to the capital account. Operating income exists when total sales revenue is greater than the cost of sales and the total operating expenses. An operating loss exists when the cost of sales and total operating expenses are greater than sales revenue. Operating income is the income before tax, and will become net income after tax is applied.

## Worksheet

A worksheet can be prepared at the end of an accounting period to ensure that all the accounts are in balance and to show all information needed to journalise adjusting and closing entries, and to prepare major financial statements. The sequence of completion of the worksheet begins with an unadjusted trial balance. End-of-period adjustments are made in the adjustment columns and then extended to the adjusted trial balance columns. Each account shown in the adjusted trial balance columns belongs to the income statement or balance sheet columns.

Sales revenue, cost of sales, and expense accounts are extended to the income statement. Assets, liabilities, and ownership equity accounts are extended to the balance sheet. The debit-credit balances of each of the five two-column sets must be equal. If any total debit and credit balances of the five two-column sets are not equal, an error has been made, and it must be corrected before continuing completion of the worksheet. If all column sets are balanced correctly, the worksheet is completed if no errors are noted.

All information is shown in the workshcet to journalise adjusting and closing entries, and to prepare the income statement and balance sheet.

The accounting cycle can be summarised in these steps:

— Perform transactional analysis. Verify documentation or information such as invoices, sales, and checks to indicate that a journal entry is required.

— Journalise. Record a business transaction in the journal.

— Post a journal entry. Transfer journal instructions to a specific account and in the amount directed.

— Prepare an unadjusted trial balance. List all ledger accounts with balances to confirm the debit-balanced accounts are equal to the credit-balanced accounts.

— Prepare a worksheet (optional). Record the unadjusted trial balance, record end-of-period adjusting entries, develop adjusted trial balance, and extend appropriate accounts to the income statement and balance sheet columns.

— Adjust the ledger accounts. Journalise and post end-of-period adjustments to the specified accounts. An unadjusted trial balance or a completed worksheet will provide needed information.

— Close the temporary accounts. Journalise and post closing entries to bring the temporary accounts to a zero balance. An adjusted trial balance or a completed worksheet shows needed information.

— Prepare a post-closing trial balance. Take information from the ledger accounts or a post-closing trial balance, or complete a worksheet to show needed information. The post-closing trial balance verifies the accuracy of the adjusting and closing procedures and confirms that all temporary accounts have been closed to a zero balance.

— Prepare the income statement. Take information from the income statement ledger accounts or from a completed worksheet and prepare an income statement in proper format.

— Prepare the balance sheet. Take information from the balance sheet ledger accounts or a post-closing trial balance, or complete a worksheet, and prepare a balance sheet in the proper format.

## Computer Applications

An understanding of basic accounting procedures and the managerial applications needed to assist management in the decision-making process is essential. Today, most hospitality businesses in hotels, motels, food service, and beverage operations are using computers to record, report, and analyse the effectiveness of internal operations and the preparation of financial statements.

Computers have, in effect, successfully removed much of the time-consuming drudgery present in a manual accounting system. The use of computers allows the creation of and updating of account ledgers, through journal entries, and provides unadjusted and adjusted trial balances of accounts, a post-closing trial balances, and financial statements.

Thus, it is essential to understand what information is needed as input to a computer system and also understand the output of information the computer is capable of providing. In essence, all of the information provided by manual procedures in the examples and exhibits can automatically be generated with a computer system set-up with a basic office oriented software system. Knowing what an average check is for a food service operation is one thing, but knowing how it is determined gives a greater insight as to how it can be changed. This simple analogy rings true for the great majority of developed ratios, percentages, units, and dollar values that can be generated through computer analysis.

Needless to say, software programmes are available for specific business operations within the hospitality industry, which can assist in safeguarding the assets, controlling cost, maximizing profit, and providing information to measure the efficiency and productivity of an operation.

# 3

# Financial Reporting

The accounting profession has established a set of standards and rules that are recognised as a general guide for financial reporting. This recognised set of standards is called generally accepted accounting principles (GAAP). Generally accepted means that these principles must have "substantial authoritative support." Such support usually comes from two standard-setting bodies: the Financial Accounting Standards Board (FASB) and the Securities and Exchange Commission (SEC).

Since the early 1970s the business and governmental communities have given the FASB the responsibility for developing accounting principles in this country. This is an ongoing process; accounting principles change to reflect changes in the business environment and in the needs of users of accounting information. Prior to the establishment of the FASB, accounting principles were developed on a problem-by-problem basis. Rule-making bodies developed accounting rules and methods to solve specific problems.

Critics charged that the problem-by-problem approach led over time to inconsistent rules and practices. No clearly developed conceptual framework of accounting existed to refer to in solving new problems. In response to these criticisms, the FASB developed a conceptual framework. It serves as the basis for resolving accounting and reporting problems. The FASB spent considerable time and effort on this project. The Board views its conceptual framework as "... a constitution, a coherent system of interrelated objectives and fundamentals." The FASB's conceptual framework consists of four items:

— Objectives of financial reporting
— Qualitative characteristics of accounting information
— Elements of financial statements
— Operating guidelines (assumptions, principles, and constraints)

### Financial Reporting Objectives

The FASB began to work on the conceptual framework by looking at the objectives of financial reporting. Determining these objectives required answers to such basic questions as: Who uses financial statements? Why? What information do they need? How knowledgeable about business and accounting are financial statement users? How should financial information be reported so that it is best understood? In answering these questions, the FASB concluded that financial reporting should have three objectives:

— The information is useful to those making investment and credit decisions.
— The financial reports are helpful in assessing future cash flows.
— The economic resources (assets), the claims to those resources (liabilities), and the changes in those resources and claims are clearly identified.

The FASB then undertook to describe the characteristics that make accounting information useful.

## Qualitative Characteristics of Financial Information

The overriding criterion for such accounting choices is decision usefulness. The accounting practice selected should be the one that generates the most useful financial information for making a decision. To be useful, information should possess the following qualitative characteristics: relevance, reliability, comparability, and consistency.

### *Relevance Information*

Accounting information has relevance if it makes a difference in a decision. Relevant information has either predictive or feedback value or both. Predictive value helps users forecast future events. For example, when Four Seasons Hotels & Resorts issues financial statements, the information in them is considered relevant because it provides a basis for predicting future earnings. Feedback value confirms or corrects prior expectations. When Four Seasons issues financial statements, it confirms or corrects prior expectations about the financial health of the company. In addition, accounting information has relevance if it is timely. It must be available to decision makers before it loses its capacity to influence decisions. If Four Seasons reported its financial information only every five years, the information would be of limited use in decision making.

### *Reliability of Information*

Reliability of information means that the information is free of error and bias. In short, it can be depended on. To be reliable, accounting information must be verifiable: We must be able to prove that it is free of error and bias. It also must be a faithful representation of what it purports to be: It must be factual. If the Felcor Lodging Trust balance sheet reports assets of $8 billion when it had assets of $51 billion, then the statement is not a faithful representation.

Finally, accounting information must be neutral: It cannot be selected, prepared, or presented to favour one set of interested users over another. To ensure reliability, certified public accountants audit financial statements.

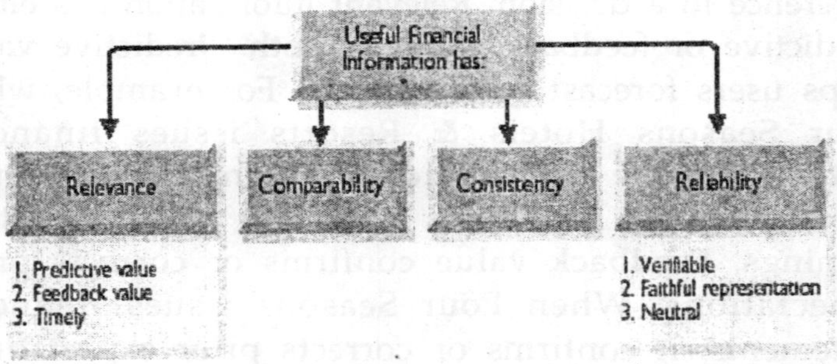


*Figure 1. The qualitative characteristics of accounting information*

## *Comparability of Information*

Accounting information about an enterprise is most useful when it can be compared with accounting information about other enterprises. Comparability results when different companies use the same accounting principles. For example, Accor and Adam's Mark use the cost principle in reporting plant assets on the balance sheet. Also, each company uses the revenue recognition and matching principles in determining its net income.

Conceptually, comparability should also extend to the methods used by companies in complying with an accounting principle. Accounting methods include the FIFO and LIFO methods of inventory costing, and various depreciation methods.

At this point, comparability of methods is not required, even for companies in the same industry. Thus, LaQuinta Inns and Suites and Choice Hotels International may use different inventory costing and depreciation methods in their financial statements.

The only accounting requirement is that each company must disclose the accounting methods used. From the disclosures, the external user can determine whether the financial information is comparable.

### *Consistency*

Consistency means that a company uses the same accounting principles and methods from year to year. If a company selects FIFO as the inventory costing method in the first year of operations, it is expected to use FIFO in succeeding years. When financial information has been reported on a consistent basis, the financial statements permit meaningful analysis of trends within a company.

A company can change to a new method of accounting. To do so, management must justify that the new method results in more meaningful financial information. In the year in which the change occurs, the change must be disclosed in the notes to the financial statements. Such disclosure makes users of the financial statements aware of the lack of consistency.

## Elements of Financial Statements

An important part of the accounting conceptual framework is a set of definitions that describe the basic terms used in accounting. The FASB refers to this set of definitions as the elements of financial statements. They include such terms as assets, liabilities, equity, revenues, and expenses.

Because these elements are so important, it is crucial that they be precisely defined and universally applied. Finding the appropriate definition for many of these elements is not easy. For example, should the value of a company's employees be reported as an asset on a balance sheet? Should the death of the company's president be reported as a loss? A good set of definitions should provide answers to these types of questions.

## Operating Guidelines of Accounting

The objectives of financial reporting, the qualitative characteristics of accounting information, and the elements of financial statements are very broad. Because practicing accountants must solve practical problems, more detailed guidelines are needed. In its conceptual framework, the FASB recognised the need for operating guidelines. Classify these guidelines as assumptions, principles, and constraints. These guidelines are well established and accepted in accounting.

Assumptions provide a foundation for the accounting process. Principles are specific rules that indicate how economic events should be reported in the accounting process. Constraints on the accounting process allow for a relaxation of the principles under certain circumstances.

## BASIC ACCOUNTING ASSUMPTIONS

Assumptions provide a foundation for the accounting process. Below are definitions of four basic accounting assumptions.

### *Monetary Unit Assumption*

The monetary unit assumption states that only transaction data that can be expressed in terms of money be included in the accounting records. For example, the value of a company president is not reported in a company's financial records because it cannot be expressed easily in dollars. An important corollary to the monetary unit assumption is the assumption that the unit of measure remains relatively constant over time.

### *Economic Entity Assumption*

The economic entity assumption states that the activities of the entity be kept separate and distinct from the activities of the owners and of all other economic entities. For example, it is assumed that the activities of Peabody Hotel Group can be distinguished from those of other computer companies such as Cendant, Forte Hotels, and John Q. Hammons Hotels.

### *Time Period Assumption*

The time period assumption states that the economic life of a business can be divided into artificial time periods. Thus, it is assumed that the activities of business enterprises such as MeriStar Hotels and Resorts, Ameri Suites, Carlson Hospitality, or any enterprise can be subdivided into months, quarters, or a year for meaningful financial reporting purposes.

### Going Concern Assumption

The going concern assumption assumes that the enterprise will continue in operation long enough to carry out its existing objectives. In spite of numerous business failures, companies have a fairly high continuance rate. It has proved useful to adopt a going concern assumption for accounting purposes.

The accounting implications of this assumption are critical. If a going concern assumption is not used, then plant assets should be stated at their liquidation value (selling price less cost of disposal)-not at their cost. In that case, depreciation and amortisation of these assets would not be needed. Each period, these assets would simply be reported at their liquidation value. Also, without this assumption, the current-noncurrent classification of assets and liabilities would not matter. Labelling anything as long-term would be difficult to justify.

Acceptance of the going concern assumption gives credibility to the cost principle. Only when liquidation appears imminent is the going concern assumption inapplicable. In that case, assets would be better stated at liquidation value than at cost.

## Principles of Accounting

On the basis of the fundamental assumptions of accounting, the accounting profession has developed principles that dictate how economic events should be recorded and reported.

### Revenue Recognition Principle

The revenue recognition principle dictates that revenue should be recognised in the accounting period in which it is earned. But applying this general principle in practice can be difficult. Some companies improperly recognise revenue on goods that have not been shipped to customers.

Similarly, until recently, financial institutions immediately recorded a large portion of their loan fees as revenue rather than spreading those fees over the life of the loan. When a sale is involved, revenue is recognised at the point of sale. This sales basis involves an exchange transaction between the seller and buyer. The sales price is an objective measure of the amount of revenue realised. However, two exceptions to the sales basis for revenue recognition have become generally accepted -the percentage-of-completion method and the instalment method. These methods are left for more advanced courses.

### *Expense Recognition*

Expense recognition is traditionally tied to revenue recognition: "Let the expense follow the revenue." It dictates that expenses be matched with revenues in the period in which efforts are made to generate revenues. Expenses are not recognised when cash is paid, or when the work is performed, or when the product is produced. Rather, they are recognised when the labour (service) or the product actually makes its contribution to revenue.

But, it is sometimes difficult to determine the accounting period in which the expense contributed to revenues. Several approaches have therefore been devised for matching expenses and revenues on the income statement. To understand these approaches, you need to understand the nature of expenses. Costs are the source of expenses.

Costs that will generate revenues only in the current accounting period are expensed immediately. They are reported as operating expenses in the income statement. Examples include costs for advertising, sales salaries, and repairs. These expenses are often called expired costs. Costs that will generate revenues in future accounting periods are recognised as assets. Examples include merchandise inventory, prepaid expenses, and plant assets. These costs represent unexpired costs. Unexpired costs become expenses in two ways:

— *Cost of goods sold:* Costs carried as merchandise inventory become expenses when the inventory is sold. They are expensed as cost of goods sold in the period when the sale occurs. Thus, there is a direct matching of expenses with revenues.

— *Operating expenses:* Other unexpired costs become operating expenses through use or consumption (as in the case of store supplies) or through the passage of time (as in the case of prepaid insurance). The costs of plant assets and other long-lived resources are expensed through rational and systematic allocation methods-periodic depreciation or amortisation. Operating expenses contribute to the revenues for the period, but their association with revenues is less direct than for cost of goods sold.

### *Full Disclosure Principle*

The full disclosure principle requires that circumstances and events that make a difference to financial statement users be disclosed. For example, most accountants would agree that hospitality companies should disclose any liability suits pending against them. Interested parties would want to be made aware of this contingent loss. Similarly, it is generally agreed that companies should disclose the major provisions of employee pension plans and long-term lease contracts. Compliance with the full disclosure principle occurs through the data in the financial statements and the information in the notes that accompany the statements. The first note in most cases is a summary of significant accounting policies. It includes, among others, the methods used for inventory costing, depreciation of plant assets, and amortisation of intangible assets.

Deciding how much disclosure is enough can be difficult. Accountants could disclose every financial event that occurs and every contingency that exists. But the benefits of providing additional information in some cases may be less than the costs of doing so. Many companies complain of an accounting standards overload. They also object to requirements that force them to disclose confidential information.

Determining where to draw the line on disclosure is not easy. One thing is certain: financial statements were much simpler years ago. In 1930, General Electric had no notes to its financial statements. Today it has more than twenty pages of notes! Why this change? A major reason is that the objectives of financial statements have changed. In the past, information was generally presented on what the business had done. Today, the objectives of financial reporting are more future-oriented. The goal is to provide information that makes it possible to predict the amounts, timing, and uncertainty of future cash flows.

### *Principles of Cost*

The cost principle dictates that assets be recorded at their cost. Cost is used because it is both relevant and reliable. Cost is relevant because it represents the price paid, the assets sacrificed, or the commitment made at date of acquisition. Cost is reliable because it is objectively measurable, factual, and verifiable. It is the result of an exchange transaction. Cost is the basis used in preparing financial statements.

The relevance of the cost principle, however, has come under criticism. After acquisition, the argument goes, the cost of an asset is not equivalent to market value or current value. Also, as the purchasing power of the dollar changes, so does the meaning associated with the dollar used as the basis of measurement. Consider the classic story about the individual who went to sleep and woke up 10 years later. Hurrying to a telephone, he called his broker and asked what his formerly modest stock portfolio was worth. He was told that he was a multimillionaire. His Starwood stock was worth $5 million, and his Hilton stock was up to $10 million. Elated, he was about to inquire about his other holdings, when the telephone operator cut in with "Your time is up. Please deposit $100,000 for the next three minutes."

Despite the inevitability of changing prices due to inflation, the accounting profession still follows the stable monetary unit assumption in preparing the primary financial statements. While admitting that some changes in prices do occur, the profession believes the unit of measure-the dollar-has remained sufficiently constant over time to provide meaningful financial information. Sometimes, the disclosure of price-level adjusted data is in the form of supplemental information that accompanies the financial statements.

## Accounting Constraints

Constraints permit a company to modify generally accepted accounting principles without reducing the usefulness of the reported information. The constraints are materiality and conservatism.

### *Materiality Relates*

Materiality relates to an item's impact on a firm's overall financial condition and operations. An item is material when it is likely to influence the decision of a reasonably prudent investor or creditor. It is immaterial if its inclusion or omission has no impact on a decision maker. In short, if the item does not make a difference in decision making, GAAP does not have to be followed. To determine the materiality of an amount, the accountant usually compares it with such items as total assets, total liabilities, and net income.

To illustrate how the materiality constraint is applied, assume that Rodriguez Co. purchases a number of low-cost plant assets, such as wastepaper baskets. Although the proper accounting would appear to be to depreciate these wastepaper baskets over their useful life, they are usually expensed immediately. This practice is justified because these costs are considered immaterial. Establishing depreciation schedules for these assets is costly and time consuming and will not make a material difference on total assets and net income. Another application of the materiality constraint would be the expensing of small tools. Some companies expense any plant assets under a specified dollar amount.

### *Conservatism in Accounting*

The conservatism constraint dictates that when in doubt, choose the method that will be least likely to overstate assets and income. It does not mean understating assets or income. Conservatism provides a reasonable guide in difficult situations: Do not overstate assets and income.

A common application of the conservatism constraint is the use of the lower of cost or market method for inventories. Inventories are reported at market value if market value is below cost. This practice results in a higher cost of goods sold and lower net income. In addition, inventory on the balance sheet is stated at a lower amount. Other examples of conservatism in accounting are the use of the last-in, firstout (LIFO) method for inventory valuation when prices are rising and the use of accelerated depreciation methods for plant assets. Both these methods result in lower asset-carrying values and lower net income than alternative methods.

## Financial Statements Presentation

Financial statements play an important role in attempting to meet the objectives of financial reporting. "Bottom line" information such as total assets and net income are useful to investors, but these single numbers lack sufficient detail for serious analysis. Investors and creditors generally find the parts of a financial statement more useful than the whole. Proper classification within the financial statements is therefore extremely important.

### *Balance Sheet*

The balance sheet is composed of three major elements: assets, liabilities, and stockholders' equity. Additional segregation within these groups, however, is considered useful to financial statement readers. If the form of organisation is a proprietorship, the term "Owner's equity" instead of Stockholders' equity is used to describe that section of the balance sheet. An account called Capital is reported in the owner's equity section of the balance sheet for a proprietorship. Capital is the owner's investment in the business. To illustrate, assume that

Sally Field invests $90,000 on July 10, 2004, to start up Birthday Balloons.

Because Sally Field owns the business and has chosen not to incorporate, common stock is not issued and net income (net loss) belongs to her. Therefore, common stock and retained earnings accounts are not needed. Instead, her capital account is increased by investments and by net income. It is decreased by withdrawals of assets for personal use and by net losses. The capital account represents Sally Field's claim to the net assets (assets less liabilities) of the company. If the form of organisation is a partnership, each partner has a separate capital account, and the owners' equity section shows the capital accounts of all the partners. For example, assume that A. Teller and B. Penn form a partnership on December 11, 2004, at which time Teller and Penn each invest $60,000.

### *Multiple-Step Income Statement*

The multiple-step income statement included the following.

- *Sales revenue section:* Presents the sales, discounts, allowances, and other related information to arrive at the net amount of sales revenue.
- *Cost of goods sold:* Indicates the cost of goods sold to produce sales.
- *Operating expense:* Provides information on both selling and administrative expenses.
- *Other revenues and gains:* Indicates revenues earned or gains resulting from nonoperating transactions.
- *Other expenses and losses:* Indicates expenses or losses incurred from nonoperating transactions.

Two additional items are income tax expense and earnings per share.

*Income taxes*

Income taxes must be paid and therefore reported for a corporation because a corporation is a legal entity separate and distinct from its owners. Proprietorships and partnerships are not separate legal entities; owners are therefore taxed directly on their business income. Stockholders are taxed only on the dividends they receive.

Corporate income taxes (or income tax expense) are reported in a separate section of the income statement, before net income. Income tax expense and the related liability for income taxes payable are recorded as part of the adjusting process, preceding financial statement preparation. Using the data above for Hallmark Hotel Brokerage, the adjusting entry for income tax expense at December 31, 2004.

*Earnings per share data*

Earnings per share data are frequently reported in the financial press and are widely used by stockholders and potential investors in evaluating the profitability of a company. Investors, especially, attempt to link earnings per share to the market price per share. Earnings per share (EPS) indicates the net income earned by each share of outstanding common stock. Thus, earnings per share is reported only for common stock.

For example, Hallmark Hotel Brokerage has net income of $109,200. Assuming that it has 54,600 shares of common stock outstanding for the year, earnings per share are $2 ($109,200 54,600). Because of the importance of earnings per share, most companies are required to report it on the face of the income statement. Generally this amount is simply reported below net income on the statement.

### *Financial Statements Analysing*

The financial statements should provide financial information that is useful for helping make sound investment and credit decisions. The condensed balance sheet and income statement of Blue Ribbon Meats, for 2004. In analysing and interpreting financial statement information, three major characteristics are generally evaluated: liquidity, profitability, and solvency. A short-term debt holder, for example, is primarily interested in the ability of a borrower to pay obligations when they become due.

The liquidity of the borrower in such a case is extremely important in assessing the safety of a loan. A longterm debt holder, however, looks to indicators such as profitability and solvency that point to the firm's ability to survive over a long period of time. Long-term debt holders analyse earnings per share, the relationship of income to total assets invested, and the amount of debt in relation to total assets to determine whether money should be lent and at what interest rate. Similarly, stockholders are interested in the profitability and solvency of a company when assessing the likelihood of dividends and the growth potential of the common stock.

### *Liquidity*

What is Blue Ribbon Meats' ability to pay its maturing obligations and meet unexpected needs for cash? The relationship between current assets and current liabilities is critical to helping answer this question. These relationships are expressed as a ratio, called the current ratio, and as a dollar amount, called working capital.

*Current ratio*: The current ratio is current assets divided by current liabilities. For Blue Ribbon Meats, Inc., the ratio is 2.23:1. This ratio means that current assets are more than two times greater than current liabilities. Bankers, other creditors, and agencies such as Dun & Bradstreet use this ratio to determine whether the company is a good credit risk. Traditionally, a ratio of 2:1 is considered to be the standard for a good credit rating. Today, however, many sound companies have current ratios of less than 2:1.

Hotel and restaurant companies normally have a 0.8:1 to 1.2:1 current ratio. With its 2.23:1 ratio, Blue Ribbon Meats' short-term debt-paying ability appears to be very favourable. From the foregoing, you might at first assume that the higher the current ratio, the better. This is not necessarily true. A very high current ratio may indicate that the company is holding more current assets than it currently needs in the business. It is possible, therefore, that the excess resources might be directed to more profitable investment opportunities.

*Working capital:* The excess of current assets over current liabilities is called working capital. For Blue Ribbon Meats, Inc., working capital is $86,000. The amount of working capital provides some indication of the company's ability to meet its existing current obligations. A large amount of working capital generally means a company can meet its current liabilities as they fall due and, if desired, pay dividends. Although no set standards exist for the level of working capital a company should maintain, the general adequacy of a company's working capital is often determined by comparing data from prior periods and from similar companies of comparable size. Blue Ribbon Meats' working capital appears adequate.

### *Profitability ratios*

Profitability ratios measure the income or operating success of an enterprise for a given period of time. Income, or the lack of it, affects the company's ability to obtain debt or equity financing and the company's ability to grow.

*Profit margin percentage*: One important ratio used to measure profitability is the profit margin percentage (or rate of return on sales. It measures the percentage of each dollar of sales that results in net income. It is calculated by dividing net income by net sales for the period. Blue Ribbon Meats, Inc.'s profit margin percentage is 3.3 percent. This ratio seems low. Much, however, depends on the type of industry. Highvolume retailers, such as grocery stores (Safeway or Kroger) or discount stores (Wal-Mart or Target), generally have a low profit margin. They make a small profit on each sale but have many sales.

*Return on assets:* In making an investment, an investor wants to know what rate of return to expect and what risks are associated with that rate of return. The greater the risk, the higher the rate of return the investor will demand on the investment. One overall measure of profitability of a company is its rate of return on assets. It is calculated by dividing net income by total assets. Blue Ribbon Meats, Inc.'s rate of return is 5.7 percent. The rate of return on assets is relatively low, which suggests that Blue Ribbon Meats might not be using its assets effectively.

*Common Stockholders' Equity:* Another widely used rate that measures profitability from the common stockholders' viewpoint is return on common stockholders' equity. This rate shows the percentage of net income earned for each dollar of owners' investment. It is calculated by dividing net income by common stockholders' equity.

In Blue Ribbon Meats, Inc.'s case, the rate of return is 23.3 percent (or 23.3 cents per dollar). Blue Ribbon Meats' return on common stockholders' equity is quite good. The reason for this high rate of return is that Blue Ribbon Meats' assets are earning a return higher than the borrowing costs the company incurs.

*Solvency*

Solvency measures the ability of an enterprise to survive over a long period of time. Long-term debt holders and stockholders are interested in a company's ability to pay periodic interest and to repay the face value of the debt at maturity.

*Debt to total assets:* One useful measure of solvency is the debt to total assets ratio. It measures the percentage of total assets that creditors, as opposed to stockholders, provide. It is calculated by dividing total debt (liabilities) by total assets, normally expressed as a percentage. Blue Ribbon Meats, Inc.'s debt to total assets ratio is 75.4 percent. Debt to total assets of 75.4 percent means that Blue Ribbon Meats' creditors have provided approximately three-quarters of its total assets.

The higher the percentage of debt to total assets, the greater the risk that the company may be unable to meet its maturing obligations. The lower the percentage, the greater the "buffer" available to creditors should the company become insolvent. In Blue Ribbon Meats' case, unless earnings are positive and very stable, the company may have too much debt.

These percentage and ratio relationships are often used in comparison with

— expected results,
— prior year results, and
— published results of other companies in the same line of business.

Conclusions based on a single year's results are hazardous at best.

### *International Transactions*

World markets are becoming increasingly intertwined. Foreigners use American computers, eat American breakfast cereals, read American magazines, listen to American rock music, watch American movies and TV shows, and drink American soda. Americans drive Japanese cars, wear Italian shoes and Scottish woolens, drink Brazilian coffee and Indian tea, eat Swiss chocolate bars, sit on Danish furniture, and use Arabian oil. The variety and volume of exported and imported goods indicates the extensive involvement of U.S. business in international trade. Many U.S. companies consider the world their market.

Firms that conduct operations in more than one country through subsidiaries, divisions, or branches in foreign countries are referred to as multinational corporations (MNCs). The accounting for such corporations is complicated because foreign currencies are involved. These international transactions must be translated into U.S. dollars.

*Differences in standards*

In the new global economy many investment and credit decisions require the analysis of foreign financial statements. Unfortunately, accounting standards are not uniform from country to country. This lack of uniformity results from differences in legal systems, in processes for developing accounting standards, in governmental requirements, and in economic environments.

*Uniformity in standards*

Efforts to obtain uniformity in international accounting practices are taking place. In 1973 the International Accounting Standards Committee (IASC) was formed by agreement of accounting organisations in the United States, the United Kingdom, Canada, Australia, France, Germany, Japan, Mexico, and the Netherlands. Its purpose is to formulate international accounting standards and to promote their acceptance worldwide.

To date, numerous standards have been issued for IASC members to introduce to their respective countries. But, the IASC has no enforcement powers, so these standards are by no means universally applied. They are, though, generally followed by the multinational companies that are audited by international public accounting firms. The foundation has been laid for progress toward greater uniformity in international accounting.

## Accounting and Financial Reporting

Although FASB sets the rules for public accounting that must be abided by the accounting profession, the hospitality industry also sets procedures and guidelines for its various segments to ensure comparability, accountability, and meaningful usage of accounting data. For new operators, these systems even act as turnkey accounting systems. This means the system has everything included and is ready to be used in operations. The three most used and well-known systems in the industry are for the lodging, foodservice, and club areas. There is currently one under development for the gaming industry.

Why are such industry-specific systems needed? If every industry follows FASB's rules, shouldn't they then have the correct accounting information? In theory, yes. However, the rules for FASB are written for the entire accounting profession. Hospitality has accounts other industries do not, and vice versa. For instance, a restaurant will not have a depletion account for an oil rig, but a restaurant does need an accumulation depreciation account for furniture, fixtures, and equipment. Even within the hospitality industry there are differences.

A hotel is different from a club and a club is different from a theme park. Hotels have rooms revenues, country clubs have membership dues, and theme parks have admissions fees. There are recommended procedures to categorise certain expenses or naming of accounts. The accounting information provided is more useful not just for the companies themselves but also for investors, creditors, and even employees.

### *Lodging Industry*

The Uniform System of Accounts for the Lodging Industry is currently in its ninth edition. Of the three systems, this is the oldest. It was first developed by the Hotel Association of New York in 1926 and was known as the Uniform System of Accounts for Hotels. From the 1930s to the 1970s, when most hotels were smaller and motor hotels (motels) were popular, there were actually two systems: the Uniform System of Accounts for Hotels and the Uniform System of Accounts for Smaller Hotels. There was also an expense dictionary where expenditures were categorised under specific accounts so that accountants and controllers could follow the allocation trail.

The ninth edition evolved with industry trends and combines all three books into a seamless system of accounts for the entire lodging industry. The Hospitality Financial and Technology Professionals (HFTP) is working with the American Hotel and Lodging Association on the next edition.

### *Food Service Industry*

The Uniform System of Accounts for Restaurants, first published in 1927, is currently in its seventh edition. It provides sample statements, analyses blueprints, classification of accounts, and an expense dictionary. The aim of this publication, like that of the lodging and club industries, is to assist operators to interpret financial results in a more meaningful manner.

### *Club Industry*

The club industry is a self-regulating industry. With its owners also being its members, accountability is of utmost importance. The Club Managers Association of America (CMAA) was formed in 1927 and published the Proposed Uniform System of Accounts for City Clubs in 1942. It was not until 1954 that the first Uniform System of Accounts for Clubs was published. The current fifth edition is known as the Uniform System of Financial Reporting for Clubs.

Similar to the hotel industry, the club industry has seen tremendous growth, especially in real estate developments. Many new residential developments also include a club, fully equipped with all amenities and services, including one, and perhaps two, golf courses for its residents.

### *Gaming Industry*

You may feel that if any industry needs a system, the casino industry should be the first one to have a set of procedures because there are such large amounts of money involved. However, the first edition of this system is still under development. Two reasons contribute to the late birth. First, both Nevada and New Jersey have strict laws governing the operations of casinos, including how money transactions should be documented.

Many states with legalised gaming have adopted the rules of Nevada and New Jersey. In addition, casinos have been using parts of the system from the lodging industry. In the current ninth edition of the system of the lodging industry, there are also sections dedicated to the casino industry, suggesting statement presentation formats and guidelines.

## Hospitality Accounting and Financial Management

### *Hotel Operations*

Operating a hotel is like being in charge of a small city. The hotel business is full of exciting moments, surprises, heartwarming stories, and also some tough workdays. If you can imagine a mayor taking care of a city, well, that is what a general manager has to do for his or her hotel. The general manager needs to have the hotel properly staffed, with the right equipment and supplies, so guests can have a wonderful experience. Hospitality is not just the name that encompasses the industry but is also the key word to success.

The role of financial management in a hotel is crucial to its success. Reduced to the simplest terms, when the money is not there, the hotel cannot open. The hotel industry really offers a fascinating career. Visit the American Hotel and Lodging Association (AH&LA) Web site (www.ahla.com) for more information about the hotel industry from national to local levels.

*Interactions with all departments*

A typical hotel is divided into departments. The bigger the hotel, the more departments it has. Most hotels have a front office that takes care of reservations and registration. There is also a housekeeping department and an engineering and maintenance department. If the hotel is a full-service property, it will have a food and beverage department, which may include restaurant, banquet, and in-room dining. Smaller properties may have their human resources and accounting functions centralised at a regional office. An accounting department at a 1,600-room convention property may have forty to fifty employees.

Regardless of how many departments and how many employees, you can see the big picture. In the hotel business, it takes teamwork to provide the ultimate quality service and product to the guests. Five hundred convention attendees staying with the hotel expect to have their rooms ready for check-in and meeting rooms available for work. They will also expect their coffee and meal breaks served on time and the banquet room decorated with their association's banner and other materials.

The group's convention organiser is not going to talk to the housekeeper, the restaurant manager, the banquet captain, or the front office separately regarding their needs. This organiser will have one point of contact with the hotel sales and catering office and this hotel manager will need to interact with all departments to communicate the pertinent information. Thus, all departments need to interact and make decisions accordingly.

*General manager and the executive committee*

As mentioned, the general manager is like the mayor of the city. He or she will work closely with the members of the executive committee to manage the hotel. The executive committee is made up of all the department heads. This group comes together for meetings to make decisions and ensure all information is relayed correctly.

The controller, the department head of the accounting department, is a member of the executive committee. Just like the general manager, the controller has to work not only with the employees in the accounting and business office, but also with all department heads. At times, while certain department heads may not need to have constant communication with one another, the controller, as the head financial management person, is required to do so.

Controllers need to know how every department performs and whether each department is making or losing money. They can do so from a simple analysis of the departmental income statement. They can then consult with department heads to point out any concerns that are shown on the financial records. This allows departments to take appropriate actions to ensure the success of the hotel. In the career ladder of a hotel, it is highly possible that a controller can one day become the general manager.

*Casino hotel*

Financial management is important in any hotel. However, it is doubly important in a casino hotel. Think of all the cash that passes through a casino on a daily basis. We are talking about thousands to millions of dollars. The exchange of cash for playing chips, the emptying of cash at slot machines and the table games, the issuing of credit to guests, even the counting of coins and paper money, has set procedures regulated by the hotels and by the law. Therefore, besides taking care of all the billing, cash, and payables of a regular hotel, the accounting functions in a casino hotel include managing all other revenue centers from all the games. This makes a controller's function more interesting and challenging.

### *Accounting Department Organisation*

There are many users of accounting and financial information. It takes quite a bit of work to make sure that records are kept properly for all parties. The organisation depends on the size of the hotel. Some hotels may not have a need for an assistant controller; some of the other functions may not exist in a hotel, such as a food and beverage department. For most limited-service hotels, the general manager may assume the function of the controller, or that function will be centralised at a district or regional office. Following is a short description of some of the accounting functions in a hotel.

*Accounts payable*

A key area in accounting, accounts payable ensures that all bills are paid on time and all discounts are taken minimizing the costs of the hotel. Accounts payable clerks work closely with the purchasing department to verify that all invoices to be paid are indeed invoices of the hotel.

*Assistant controller*

In a big hotel, you may see one, or a few, assistant controllers. In smaller hotels, there may not be any. The controller divides the various functions to be performed so that the workload will be even. For example, one assistant might be responsible for daily transactions while another works on special projects, budgets, analyses, and the like.

*Guest and city ledgers*

A hotel keeps two ledgers: the guest ledger is associated with the guests staying at the hotel while the city ledger contains all other billings. It is important that the accounting department has a person in accounts receivable working with the city ledger so the hotel is able to bill and collect revenues due.

*Night audit*

Night auditors get their name because of the hours they work. At the end of the day after most hotel guests have retired, these auditors begin recording charges to guests' accounts and verifying the revenue for the hotel. However, with computers and various technologies, the hotel industry can post charges instantaneously. Some hotels have actually changed the night auditors to become day auditors.

*Banquet auditor*

Besides revenues charged to guest rooms, a large hotel earns the bulk of its food and beverage revenues through banquets. The banquet auditor's function is to verify the correct revenue for billing. This individual works closely with the banquet staff, the sales office staff, and the accounts receivable clerks.

*Credit*

A big hotel may have its own credit manager whose function is to check and grant credit. In today's business world, many transactions are done on credit rather than cash or cashier checks. It is, therefore, the credit manager's responsibility to conduct such investigations to be sure that a person or company is creditworthy.

***Food and beverage controller***

This is a fun and challenging position, as it has both accounting and food and beverage components. While performing all analyses of food cost percentage, yields on meat, and menu costings, the food and beverage controller also works with the chef to design new menu items, taste new products, and even be a mystery diner to taste-test the menus in other foodservice establishments.

*Front-office cashiers*

The duties of a front-office cashier are often incorporated with the front-office personnel. When guests check out, it is the duty of these cashiers to charge the guests the correct amount and secure a form of payment.

*General cashier*

Pause for a minute and think how many cash banks there are in a large hotel: a few at the front office, at least one in the restaurant, at least one in the gift shop, and so on. The general cashier is the person who is in charge of all the cash banks in the hotel. He or she also makes all deposits of checks and credit card receipts.

*Operations analyst*

This is a nice position to have in a hotel. An operation analyst performs analyses to help managers operate the hotel more effectively. From guests' statistics to revenue trends, the operations analyst does it all. However, not all hotels are able to afford an analyst on the payroll. If this is the case, an assistant controller often performs these duties. For smaller hotels where there is not an accounting office on the property, this function is done at the regional level.

*Payroll*

Payroll employees calculate the pay rate with the hours worked to do the payroll so paychecks are released on time. Payroll functions also include filing all payroll taxes and tip credits for tipped employees, as well as keeping track of vacation, sick pay, and other payroll-related deductions.

*Systems manager*

The various accounting functions cover the entire hotel operation, the systems manager or systems analyst, whose job is to take care of all technology issues, is normally founded within the accounting department. In a smaller hotel, the controller or an assistant controller may take on this responsibility. Normally, this position is found at a regional or corporate level and systems analysts will be dispatched to assist the property when needed.

### *Independent Restaurant*

The controller of an independent restaurant or a foodservice operation is similar to that of a food and beverage controller at a hotel.

The difference is that the foodservice controller concentrates on only the food and beverage side, whereas a hotel controller oversees various departments of a hotel. Therefore, besides labour cost and overhead items, accounting and financial management in the foodservice business is focused on yield analysis, food and beverage cost control, and the purchasing function.

#### *Purchasing and yield analysis*

Foodservice operations purchase food, beverages, and other items on a day-today basis. In the case of food and beverage, because products are perishable, buying the right amount of food, at the right quality, at the right time, reduces the amount of cash tied in inventory. The extra cash then provides more liquidity to the business.

When buying food and beverage, yield is important. A good-quality piece of beef may have less trimmings, yielding the foodservice operation more meat products to be sold. A can of tomatoes may just look like another can. But if the controller performs a "can-cutting" and compares the two brands, he or she might discover that one is better than the other and the cost difference might work to the advantage of the operation.

### *Food and beverage cost analysis*

In general, for a restaurant or operation that sells alcoholic beverages (liquor, beer, and wine), it is not unusual to have 15 to 30 percent of its total sales derived from beverages. This means 70 to 85 percent of the sales are made from food items. For smaller restaurants and quick-service operations that do not sell alcoholic beverages, all revenue comes from food sales. Therefore, the accounting department spends a lot of time tracking food costs. This is especially important because foodservice operations use products where prices often fluctuate.

Restaurants and operations that sell alcoholic beverages will also track beverage costs and perform various analyses. Do not think for a minute that because beverage sales are only 15 percent of total sales they are not important. First, the restaurant business is a "penny" business. One needs to watch for any penny that is earned or spent; otherwise, the profit margin can easily disappear if the business is not managed wisely. More important, the markup of beverages is very high. A bottle of wine that can be purchased retail for $15 can be sold at the restaurant from $40 to $60, depending on the type of restaurant.

Thus, careful cost analysis provides foodservice operators with useful information for product purchasing and pricing to maximize profits, while offering guests the products they prefer and enjoy. For those who are interested in the restaurant segment.

### *Club segment*

The club segment of the hospitality industry in North America is substantial. In every major city there are many country clubs. But clubs are not just country clubs. They also include city clubs, yacht clubs, racquet clubs, tennis clubs, other athletic clubs, military clubs, and university clubs. These private clubs are membership-only operations.

In 2001, The Club Managers Association of America reported more than 11,000 private clubs in the United States. Since these clubs are restrictive of clientele, the way business is carried out and, thus, the way accounting is performed is quite different from the foodservice and hotel segments of the hospitality industry.

While hotels have rooms, food, beverage, and other miscellaneous revenues, and restaurants have food, beverage, and other revenues, clubs have all of these and a unique revenue category-membership dues. Membership dues from country clubs often make up to 50 percent of a club's revenue, while food and beverage percentage is about 35 percent, with other revenues of 15 percent or so rounding up the 100 percent. These other revenues can include athletic fees for guests, golf greens fees for guests, and sales of merchandise in pro shops and gift stores.

In city clubs, food and beverage revenues often exceed that of membership, as golf membership is normally not provided in a city club environment. Membership revenues are the main source of funds needed for a club to run its operations.

# 4

# Financial Statements

In the modern capitalist system, most governments require publicly-traded companies to issue a set of documents each year called financial statements or financial reports. This set most often consists of the "balance sheet", the "income statement", the "statement of retained earnings", and the "statement of cash flows", in addition to supplementary notes and management discussion. In the United States, publicly-traded companies are required to prepare based on generally accepted accounting principles.

— *Balance sheet*: also referred to as statement of financial position or condition, reports on a company's assets, liabilities and net equity as of a given point in time.

— *Income statement*: also referred to as Profit or loss statement, reports on a company's results of operations over a period of time.

— *Statement of retained earnings*: explains the changes in a company's retained earnings over the reporting period.

— *Statement of cash flows*: reports on a company's cash flow activities, particularly its operating, investing and financing activities.

For large corporations, these statements are often complex and may include an extensive set of notes to the financial statements and management discussion and analysis. The notes typically describe each item on the balance sheet, income statement and cash flow statement in further detail. Notes to financial statements are considered an integral part of the financial statements.

The objective of financial statements is to provide information about the financial strength, performance and changes in financial position of an enterprise that is useful to a wide range of users in making economic decisions." Financial statements should be understandable, relevant, reliable and comparable. Reported assets, liabilities and equity are directly related to an organisation's financial position. Reported income and expenses are directly related to an organisation's financial performance.

Financial statements are intended to be understandable by readers who have "a reasonable knowledge of business and economic activities and accounting and who are willing to study the information diligently." Financial statements are used by a diverse group of parties, both inside and outside a business. Generally, these users are:

— *Internal Users*: are owners, managers, employees and other parties who are directly connected with a company. Owners and managers require financial statements to make important business decisions that affect its continued operations. Financial analysis are then performed on these statements to provide management with a more detailed understanding of the figures. These statements are also used as part of management's report to its stockholders, as it form part of its Annual Report. Employees also need these reports in making collective bargaining agreements

(CBA) with the management, in the case of labour unions or for individuals in discussing their compensation, promotion and rankings.

— *External Users*: are potential investors, banks, government agencies and other parties who are outside the business but need financial information about the business for a diverse number of reasons. Prospective investors make use of financial statements to assess the viability of investing in a business. Financial analyses are often used by investors and is prepared by professionals (financial analysts), thus providing them with the basis in making investment decisions. Financial institutions (banks and other lending companies) use them to decide whether to grant a company with fresh working capital or extend debt securities (such as a long-term bank loan or debentures) to finance expansion and other significant expenditures. Government entities (tax authorities) need financial statements to ascertain the propriety and accuracy of taxes and other duties declared and paid by a company. Media and the general public are also interested in financial statements for a variety of reasons.

## Audit of Financial Statements

Although the legal statutes may differ from country to country, an audit of financial statements are usually, but not exclusively required for investment, financing, and tax purposes. These are usually performed by independent accountants or auditing firms. Results of the audit are summarised in an audit report that either provide an unqualified opinion on the financial statements or qualifications as to its fairness and accuracy. The audit opinion on the financial statements is usually included in the annual report.

There has been much legal debate over who an auditor is liable to. Since audit reports tend to be addressed to the current shareholders, it is commonly thought that they owe a legal duty of care to them. But this may not be the case as determined by common law precedent.

In Canada, auditors are liable only to investors using a prospectus to buy shares in the primary market. In the United Kingdom, they have been held liable to potential investors when the auditor was aware of the potential investor and how they would use the information in the financial statements. Nowadays auditors tend to include in their report liability restricting language, discouraging anyone other than the addressees of their report from relying on it. Liability is an important issue: in the UK, for example, auditors have unlimited liability.

In the United States, especially in the post-Enron era there has been substantial concern about the accuracy of financial statements. Corporate officers (the chief executive officer (CEO) and chief financial officer (CFO)) are personally liable for attesting that financial statements "do not contain any untrue statement of a material fact or omit to state a material fact necessary to make the statements made, in light of the circumstances under which such statements were made, not misleading with respect to the period covered by the report".

Making or certifying misleading financial statements exposes the people involved to substantial civil and criminal liability. For example Bernie Ebbers (former CEO of WorldCom) was sentenced to 25 years in federal prison for allowing WorldCom's revenues to be overstated by $11 billion over five years.

### *Standards and Regulations*

Different countries have developed their own accounting principles over time, making international comparisons of companies difficult. To ensure uniformity and comparability between financial statements prepared by different companies, a set of guidelines and rules are used. Commonly referred to as Generally Accepted Accounting Principles (GAAP), these set of guidelines provide the basis in the preparation of financial statements.

Recently there has been a push towards standardising accounting rules made by the International Accounting Standards Board ("IASB"). IASB develops International Financial Reporting Standards that have been adopted by Australia, Canada and the European Union (for publicly quoted companies only), are under consideration in South Africa and other countries. The United States Federal Accounting Standards Board has made a commitment to converge the U.S. GAAP and IFRS over time.

### *Inclusion in Annual Reports*

To entice new investors, most public companies assemble their financial statements on fine paper with pleasing graphics and photos in an annual report to shareholders, attempting to capture the excitement and culture of the organisation in a "marketing brochure" of sorts. Usually the company's chief executive will write a letter to shareholders, describing management's performance and the company's financial highlights.

In the United States, prior to the advent of the internet, the annual report is considered the most effective way for corporations to communicate with individual shareholders. Blue chip companies went to great expense to produce and mail out attractive annual reports to every shareholder. The annual report was often prepared in the style of a coffee table book.

## Balance Sheet

In financial accounting, a balance sheet or statement of financial position is a summary of the value of all assets, liabilities and owners' equity for an organisation or individual on a specific date, such as the end of its financial year. A balance sheet is often described as a "snapshot" of a company's financial condition on a given date. Of the four basic financial statements, the balance sheet is the only statement which applies to a single point in time, instead of a period of time.

A company balance sheet has three parts: assets, liabilities and shareholders' equity. The main categories of assets are usually listed first and are followed by the liabilities. The difference between the assets and the liabilities is known as the net assets or the net worth of the company. According to the accounting equation, net worth must equal assets minus liabilities. Records of the values of each account or line in the balance sheet are usually maintained using a system of accounting known as the double-entry bookkeeping system.

A simple business operating entirely in cash could measure its profits by simply withdrawing the entire bank balance at the end of the period, plus any cash in hand. However, real businesses are not paid immediately; they build up inventories of goods to sell and they acquire buildings and equipment.

### *Kinds of Balance Sheets*

A balance sheet summarises an organisation or

individual's asset, equity and liabilities at a specific point in time. Individuals and small businesses tend to have simple balance sheets. [*dead link*] Larger businesses tend to have more complex balance sheets, and these are presented in the organisation's annual report. Large businesses also may prepare balance sheets for segments of their businesses. A balance sheet often *compares* two balance sheets for a single organisation.

### *Personal balance sheet*

A personal balance sheet lists current assets such as cash in checking accounts and savings accounts, long-term assets such as common stock and real estate, current liabilities such as loan debt and mortgage debt due or overdue, and long-term liabilities such as mortgage and other loan debt. Securities and real estate values are listed at market value rather than at historical cost or cost basis. Personal net worth is the difference between an individual's total assets and total liabilities.

### *Small business balance sheet*

A small business balance sheet lists current assets such as cash, accounts receivable, and inventory, fixed assets such as land, buildings, and equipment, intangible assets such as patents, and liabilities such as accounts payable, accrued expenses, and long-term debt. Contingent liabilities such as warranties are noted in the footnotes to the balance sheet. The small business's equity is the difference between total assets and total liabilities.

## ***Corporate Balance Sheet Structure***

Guidelines for corporate balance sheets are given by the International Accounting Standards Committee and numerous country-specific organisations. Balance sheet account names and usage depend on the organisation's country and the type of organisation. Government organisations do not generally follow standards established for individuals or businesses.

*Shareholders equity*

The net assets shown by the balance sheet equals the third part of the balance sheet, which is known as the shareholders' equity. Formally, shareholders' equity is part of the company's liabilities: they are funds "owing" to shareholders (after payment of all other liabilities); usually, however, "liabilities" is used in the more restrictive sense of liabilities excluding shareholders' equity.

The balance of assets and liabilities (including shareholders' equity) is not a coincidence. Records of the values of each account in the balance sheet are maintained using a system of accounting known as double-entry bookkeeping. In this sense, shareholders' equity by construction must equal assets minus liabilities, and are a residual.

— numbers of shares authorised, issued and fully paid, and issued but not fully paid
— par value of shares
— reconciliation of shares outstanding at the beginning and the end of the period
— description of rights, preferences, and restrictions of shares
— treasury shares, including shares held by subsidiaries and associates

— shares reserved for issuance under options and contracts

— a description of the nature and purpose of each reserve within owners' equity

## Income Statement

An Income Statement, also called a Profit and Loss Statement (P&L), is a financial statement for companies that indicates how Revenue (money received from the sale of products and services before expenses are taken out, also known as the "top line") is transformed into net income (the result after all revenues and expenses have been accounted for, also known as the "bottom line").

The purpose of the income statement is to show managers and investors whether the company made or lost money during the period being reported. In reference to charitable organisations, an income statement is called a Statement of Activities and Changes in Net Assets.

Income statements should help investors and creditors determine the past performance of the enterprise; predict future performance; and assess the risk of achieving future cash flows. However, information in an income statement has several limitations:

— items that might be relevant but cannot be reliably measured are not reported (e.g. brand recognition and loyalty)

— some numbers depend on accounting methods used (e.g. using FIFO or LIFO accounting to measure inventory level)

— some numbers depend on judgments and estimates (e.g. depreciation expense depends on estimated useful life and salvage value).

***Items on Income Statement***

*Operating section*

— Net Revenue - Inflows or other enhancements of assets of an entity or settlements of its liabilities during a period from delivering or producing goods, rendering services, or other activities that constitute the entity's ongoing major or central operations. Usually presented as sales minus sales discounts, returns, and allowances.

— Expenses - Outflows or other using-up of assets or incurrence of liabilities during a period from delivering or producing goods, rendering services, or carrying out other activities that constitute the entity's ongoing major or central operations.

  — Cost of goods sold - represents the amount a product costs to produce

  — General and administrative expenses (G & A) - represent expenses to manage the business (officer salaries, legal and professional fees, utilities, insurance, depreciation of office building and equipment, stationery, supplies)

  — Selling expenses - represent expenses needed to sell products (e.g., sales salaries and commissions, advertising, freight, shipping, depreciation of sales equipment)

  — R & D expenses - represent expenses included in research and development

  — Depreciation - represents costs associated with depreciated assets

*Non-operating section*

— Other revenues or gains - revenues and gains from other than primary business activities (e.g. rent, patents). It also includes unusual gains and losses that are either unusual or infrequent, but not both (e.g. sale of securities or fixed assets).

— Other expenses or losses - expenses or losses not related to primary business operations.

*Irregular items*

They are reported separately because this way users can better predict future cash flows - irregular items most likely won't happen next year. These are reported net of taxes.

— Discontinued operations is the most common type of irregular items. Shifting business location, stopping production temporarily, or changes due to technological improvement do not qualify as discontinued operations.

— Extraordinary items are both unusual (abnormal) and infrequent, for example, unexpected nature disaster, expropriation, prohibitions under new regulations. Note: natural disaster might not qualify depending on location (e.g. frost damage would not qualify in Canada but would in the tropics).

— Changes in accounting principle is, for example, changing method of computing depreciation from straight-line to sum-of-the-years'-digits. However, changes in estimates (e.g. estimated useful life of a fixed asset) do not qualify.

*Earnings per share*

Because of its importance, earnings per share (EPS) are required to be disclosed on the face of the income statement. A company which reports any of the irregular items must also report EPS for these items either in the statement or in the notes.

## Statement of Retained Earnings

The statement of retained earnings also known as "statement of owner's equity" and "statement of net assets" for non-profit organisations, is one of the basic financial statements as per Generally Accepted Accounting Principles, and it explains the changes in company's retained earnings over the reporting period. It breaks down changes affecting the account, such as profits or losses from operations, dividends paid, and any other items charged or credited to retained earnings. A retained earnings statement is required by Generally Accepted Accounting Principles (GAAP) whenever comparative balance sheets and income statements are presented. It may appear in the balance sheet, in a combined income statement and changes in retained earnings statement, or as a separate schedule.

Therefore, the statement of retained earnings uses information from the income statement and provides information to the balance sheet. Retained earnings are part of the balance sheet (another basic financial statement) under "stockholders equity", and is mostly affected by net income earned during a period of time by the company less any dividends paid to the company's owners/stockholders. The retained earnings account on the balance sheet is said to represent an "accumulation of earnings" since net profits and losses are added/ subtracted from the account from period to period.

The general equation can be expressed as following:

Ending Retained Earnings = Beginning Retained Earnings - Investments - Dividends Paid + Net Income

## Cash Flow Statement

In financial accounting, a cash flow statement or

statement of cash flows is a financial statement that shows a company's incoming and outgoing money (sources and uses of cash) during a time period (often monthly or quarterly). The statement shows how changes in balance sheet and income accounts affected cash and cash equivalents, and breaks the analysis down according to operating, investing, and financing activities. As an analytical tool the statement of cash flows is useful in determining the short-term viability of a company, particularly its ability to pay bills. International Accounting Standard 7 (IAS 7), is the International Accounting Standard that deals with cash flow statements.

People and groups interested in cash flow statements include

— accounting personnel, who need to know whether the organisation will be able to cover payroll and other immediate expenses

— potential lenders or creditors, who want a clear picture of a company's ability to repay

— potential investors, who need to judge whether the company is financially sound

— potential employees or contractors, who need to know whether the company will be able to afford compensation

The cash flow statement was previously known as the statement of changes in financial position or flow of funds statement. The cash flow statement reflects a firms liquidity or solvency.

The balance sheet is a snapshot of a firm's financial resources and obligations at a single point in time, and the income statement summarises a firm's financial transactions over an interval of time. These two financial statements reflect the accrual basis accounting used by firms to match revenues with the expenses associated with generating those revenues. The cash flow statement includes only inflows and outflows of cash and cash equivalents; it excludes transactions that do not directly affect cash receipts and payments. These noncash transactions include depreciation and write-offs on bad debts. The cash flow statement is a cash basis report on three types of financial activities: operating activities, investing activities, and financing activities. Noncash activities are usually reported in footnotes.

The cash flow statement is intended to provide information on a firm's liquidity and solvency and its ability to change cash flows in future circumstances provide additional information for evaluating changes in assets, liabilities and equity improve the comparability of different firms' operating performance by eliminating the effects of different accounting methods indicate the amount, timing and probability of future cash flows. The cash flow statement has been adopted as a standard financial statement because it eliminates allocations which might be derived from different accounting methods, such as various timeframes for depreciating fixed assets.

### *Cash Flow Statement*

The cash flow statement is partitioned into cash flow resulting from operating activities, cash flow resulting from investing activities, and cash flow resulting from financing activities.

#### *Operating activities*

Operating activities include the production, sales and delivery of the company's product as well as collecting payment from its customers. This could include purchasing raw materials, building inventory, advertising and shipping the product.

Under IAS 7, operating cash flows include

— receipts from the sale of goods or services
— receipts for the sale of loans, debt or equity instruments in a trading portfolio
— interest received on loans
— dividends received on equity securities
— payments to suppliers for goods and services
— payments to employees or on behalf of employees
— tax payments
— interest payments (alternatively, this can be reported under financing activities in IAS 7, but not in US GAAP)
— payments for the sale of loans, debt or equity instruments in a trading portfolio

Items which are added back to the net income figure (which is found on the Income Statement) to arrive at cash flows from operations generally include:

— Depreciation (loss of tangible asset value over time)
— Deferred tax
— Amortisation (loss of intangible asset value over time)
— Any gains or losses associated with an asset sale (unrealised gains/losses are also added back from the income statement)

### *Investing Activities*

Investing activities focus on the purchase of the long-term assets a company needs in order to make and sell its products, and the selling of any long-term assets.

Under IAS 7, investing cash flows include

- collections on loan principal and sales of other firms' debt instruments
- investment returns from other firms' equity instruments, including sale of those instruments
- receipts from sale of plant and equipment
- expenditure for purchase of plant and equipment
- loans made and acquisition of other firms' debt instruments
- expenditure for purchase of other firms' equity instruments (unless held for trading or considered cash equivalents)

Items under investing activities include:

- Capital expenditures, which include purchases (and sales) of property, plant and equipment
- Investments

# 5

# Budgeting

Today's hotel companies are more competitive and dynamic than ever before. As a result, the days when hotel budgeting was merely a routine process of incrementally increasing the prior year revenues and expenses have long ended. Successful hospitality companies are constantly seeking ways to improve their ability to predict future operations and related resource requirements, enabling them to adjust their budget plans as needed to stay ahead of the competition. Not only does this alter the importance of the budget and forecast process; but, it also changes the traditional methods used of incremental, fixed and flexible budgeting processes.

The hospitality industry's traditional method of budgeting revenues and expenses has been the same for decades. Up to now, the most commonly used methods have been Incremental Budgeting and Fixed or Flexible Budgeting.

*Incremental Budgeting*: this method is widely used in the hospitality industry and generally entails budgeting revenues and expenses based on the prior period adjusting for inflation by a percentage.

*Fixed and Flexible Budgeting* is usually for one specific expense item that is referred to as 'fixed'. A budget adjusted for a change in the level of activity is called a 'flexed' or 'flexible' budget, which means that when the level of activity changes, it is expected that the total of all costs will change. Information about how each type of cost behaves is related to how income enables budgets to be adjusted for different levels of activity. If actual results are to be compared with budgets for the purposes of performance measurement.

Hotels most often budget simply by increasing the Key Performance Indicators (KPI) by a targeted percentage or by a given CPI index on a monthly basis, and then calling it a day without any of the necessary detailed explanations to support these expenses. Such budgeting and forecasting methods have created a tremendous short fall in future projections that put owners in a difficult situation when confronted by investors and lenders.

Over the past few years, however, tremendous technological improvements have been made to enhance revenue budgeting tools. There are now a few revenue yield management systems available to improve ADR, market penetration and RevPar. This has helped many hospitality companies improve market share, penetration and hotel positioning in each market. So it would also seem that with all the new technology available it should be easy for hoteliers to use the more informative Zero Base Budgeting method.

## Zero Based Budgeting Process

Zero based budgeting derives from the idea that such budgets are developed from a zero base; that is, at the beginning of the budget process, all budget accounts have a value of Zero. This is in sharp contrast to the incremental budgeting system where generally a new budget tends to start with a balance at least equal to last year's total balance, or an estimate of it.

The goal of preparing a zero base budget is to achieve an optimal allocation of resources that incremental and other budgeting methods are less likely to present. Zero Based Budgeting starts by asking managers to identify and justify their area(s) of work in terms of business volumes. Zero Based Budgeting forces managers to justify their work by saying to them that unless and until they put forward a budget that more senior management can support, at least to a large extent; then the budget will not be approved. If Zero Based Budgeting is applied as literally as it is designed, then unjustified work and expenses would simply stop.

An effective zero base budgeting system benefits organizations in several ways. It will:

— Focus the budget process on a comprehensive analysis of objectives and needs

— Combine planning and budgeting into a single process

— Cause managers to evaluate in detail the cost effectiveness of their operations

— Expand management participation in planning and budgeting at all levels of the organization

Zero Based Budgeting process has a lot to offer it in terms of the way it forces management at all levels of an organization to become involved in the budgeting process. Zero Based Budgeting is built on the concept that what one expects in the future will be dependant on the ability to persuade the rest of the management team that it is deserved.

***Advantages***

1. Results in efficient allocation of resources as it is based on needs and benefits.
2. Drives managers to find out cost effective ways to improve operations.

3. Detects inflated budgets.
4. Useful for service department where the output is difficult to identify.
5. Increases staff motivation by providing greater initiative and responsibility in decision-making.
6. Increases communication and coordination within the organization.
7. Identifies and eliminates wastage and obsolete operations.

*Disadvantages*

1. Forced to justify every detail related to expenditure.
2. Difficult to implement using spreadsheets (would require a database application to be most effective).
3. It is very time-consuming if justification sheets are done using spreadsheets.
4. Necessary to train managers on the concept. Zero Based Budgeting should be clearly understood by managers at various levels otherwise it cannot be successfully implemented.
5. Difficult to administer and communicate the budgeting process because more managers are involved in the process.

Hotel owners are looking for detailed justification of how each dollar is spent and how well their asset is managed. The understanding of expenses and their relationship to the revenues, room nights, food covers and other business indicators that affect profitability is critical, and the lack of documentation explaining this relationship can make the process a very tedious one.

A good budget package should eliminate the old fashion spreadsheet budgets and give operators the flexibility to create different scenarios and associate each expense as it relates to the business. This is necessary because in the hospitality industry, expenses are constantly increasing while the revenue streams are highly variable. Database budgets will not only facilitate the preparation of zero based budgets and forecasts, but also will assist operators with providing sufficient detailed information for the hotel owners and asset managers when reviewing the annual budgets and the monthly forecasts.

It is time for hotel companies and individual hotel operators to break the paradigm of budgeting by spreadsheets and seek for the technological help to get up to speed with the tools that will help provide accurate information... Budgeting by spreadsheets is the way of the past and inaccuracy is the most likely outcome.

A budget/forecast with sufficient supporting documentation will be most likely approved faster. The variances to actual would be then easier to explain and easier to manage than a budget prepared by simple marginal increases over prior years. It is time to make department managers part of the planning process and accountable for their budgets and forecast instead of the usual process where hotel controllers are expected to the do all of this alone.

General Managers must involve all departments when preparing monthly forecast and annual budgets. It is time for hotel departmental managers to be business partners instead of just being told how to run their operations and accountability should be part of everyone's performance. The Hospitality industry is behind time, behind the other industries and behind in technology when it comes to way of budget and forecast the future so is time to shift the paradigm and move to a better database solution.

## ABCD's of the Re-Budgeting Game

In the wake of September 11th tragedy, most hotel

companies are re-doing their budgets and guessing, as best they can, the potential of their hotels in different markets throughout the US. This new budgeting process will be successful if hotels take into account the four variables that predicate the accuracy of their numbers. This will call as ABCD's of the re-budgeting game:

***A is for ability of the Sales Team***

This is the wrong time to push and frustrate the sales staff. Management needs to clarify the plan and facilitate the execution process by creating and maintaining a positive climate of direction and support. No need for drama. Everyone knows that it is tough it is out there and the last thing any property wants to is discourage the sales force by giving them unachievable goals and an insurmountable amount of reporting. The plan, whether it is a higher volume of negotiated corporate accounts at lower rates or group business to fill in specific shoulder dates, should be challenging but achievable. A budget is as challenging as the sales team is able to deliver against it.

***B is for best data***

The data that each property should focus on is the one affecting their immediate market. External and internal statistics are vital for this budgeting process. In the corporate segment, for instance, each hotel should have a full grasp of what volume each of their local corporate accounts is bringing to the area next year. In the leisure segment, each hotel may need to reassess how this market segment reaches their particular location and property.

In the past, leisure clientele drove approximately two hours to reach a destination. Now research is showing that they may drive as much as 5 or 6 hours to avoid flying. This information as well as other external and internal statistics may make the difference between a realistic budget and a guessing game. The outcome of each property's budget is predicated on the accuracy and usefulness of the best available data they've collected and studied.

### *C is for Competitor's Strategies and Actions*

If a hotel is in a market place where everyone is discounting to gain business, they will be forced to budget low rates to ensure they are still in the bidding game for group and transient business. To better understand the competition most hotels must go beyond the monthly STAR report and study the weekly trends of the E-STAR.

The Hotelligence provides good data but it does not tell anyone how low the competition is bidding for next year's RFP's. Each hotel must keep a close eye on group rate biddings and rack rates quoted for future reservation dates to be able to estimate the strategy of their competitive set. Much of what the competition is doing is unknown at this time and this will affect the accuracy of the new budget.

### *D is for Demand Level*

The additional supply in 2000 had little impact, if any, in several markets due to the exponential increase in both occupancy and average daily rates. Today, even though increased supply is not a threat in most parts of the country, the demand have fallen off the charts. Many hotels can see that in house reservation volume of incoming calls have dropped tremendously. To predict when this trend will reverse is a hard guess.

Today several hotels are acquiring low rated business to build occupancy for next year. Their plan is to have a base on which they are able to gain more business at a higher rate. The challenge, however, is in the demand factor. If these hotels fall in an area that does not gain a substantial increase in demand, they will find themselves discounting the remainder of their inventory against an unachievable budget. In closing next year's budget should be realistically challenging with zero fat in expenses. Hotels should "dollarize" each of their expense lines in the budget to make certain they are maximizing the potential of their property in their respective location.

## Cost of Capital and its Impact

Never having had enough capital to take advantage of all the various opportunities to grow that have presented themselves. The less you have, the costlier it is and the harder it is to get. Capital for hotel ventures typically consists of two components, debt and equity. Their costs are the interest on the debt, the investors' expected return on equity and the cost of obtaining the capital itself. Some of the cost of raising capital can initially be folded back into the debt or equity but in the end it is paid for with additional interest or less profit distribution.

The cost of debt actually includes several different components. Among the possible components are mortgage origination fees, mortgage brokerage commissions, points, prepayment penalties, legal fees, appraisal fee, environmental study fee, and finally interest. The component with the most impact over time is interest. Interest rates charged for commercial mortgages are impacted by a number of factors. These might include, but are not limited to, the term of the loan, whether the interest rate is variable or fixed, the basis on which the variable interest moves and the amount it can fluctuate in any one period, interest rates at the time the loan commitment is made, the actual source of the funds the lender will be using to make the mortgage loan and a lot of issues that are purely subjective..

These subjective items include the lender's perception of these items: the risk of the hotel project relative to the other loans that could be made; the ultimate value of the collateral; the financial stability of the borrowing entity and its principals; quality of management; and if the project "fits" in the lender's loan portfolio relative to the type of project it is. Where the lender stands relative to achieving their lending goals for the time period and the political strength of the particular person carrying the loan through the underwriting process are also major factors.

Aside from looking at debt coverage ratios and loan to value ratios the lender is going to consider all these other factors at some level. They will all ultimately affect the amount of the loan and the terms. Every aspect of the terms has a relative cost to the borrower. For instance a lender may make the borrower escrow funds to complete certain required improvements in the hotel.

Distribution of those funds will not be done until they receive all documentation that the improvements are completed, paid for and lien releases obtained. This means the borrower has to come up with the funds from other sources until the lender releases the funds. There is a cost to those additional funds, either additional interest or opportunity cost because they are not invested elsewhere.

If the escrow agreement is written so that the bank will pay for the improvements from the escrow fund as they are completed the borrower may not have to come up with as much extra money. The lender, however, is now assuming some risk that the projects will, in fact, be completed. For this to work efficiently for the lender, borrower and contractors, the escrow agreements and contracts for construction all have to be coordinated to all parties' satisfaction. The cost of coordinating these items will show up as time, legal fees and probably higher prices from the contractor.

The point here is that a hotel developer with sufficient capital does not have to do these things or bear these costs. This savings increases the return on the investment as compared to a developer with less capital. If the lender perceives one borrower and his or her project to be less risky than another's they may grant more favourable terms in the loan in the form of slightly lower interest.

On the surface the impact of this may not be significant but the reality is quite different. For instance on a $10,000,000 project with a $7,500,000 mortgage for 20 years the difference between an interest rate of 8.5% and 8.25% is $14,184 in principal and interest payments. If one disregards the tax implications of this and only evaluates the cash on cash return on equity the difference is just over a half a percentage point.

If the investors were going to receive an average cash on cash return on equity from operations of 19.65% with the 8.5% percent interest rate they will now receive one of 20.217%. Which developer will have the easier time raising equity capital? Among other things easier means less costly. And less costly also translates into even higher returns on equity.

While one doesn't usually think of equity as having a cost it does. In the simplest terms an individual investor has choices as to where s/he might invest. These alternatives all have different levels of expected return and risk. The higher the perceived risk the higher the expected return. If this investor could have invested in a government backed security and had a return of 6.0% without risk then their perceived cost is at least that amount. If they are going to take the risk of investing in something they know nothing about, have no control over and which has no liquidity they are going to have a much higher expectation for their investment return.

The developer is probably going to have to forego some return until the investors' expectations are met. This is a cost of capital to the developer. Another example might be when the developer is larger and decides to go to the public for the equity. Whether the approach is through a registered private placement memorandum or a small stock offering there will be significant legal, accounting and other fees associated with the fund raising project. Depending on the planned source of funds, the size of the fund raising has to be greater than a certain amount to justify these methods.

On the other hand a major publicly traded REIT (Real Estate Investment Trust) or C corporation has already gone to this expense. So much money, hundreds of millions or more, has been raised that the cost of the funds is relatively low relative to interest rates. Such a company will simply buy a hotel for cash from their cash reserves or credit lines in a very short process and if appropriate get a mortgage at their leisure on very favourable terms.

Because they were able to act quickly and pay all cash to the seller this buyer probably obtained much more favourable terms on the purchase. As a further point, because their cost of capital was so much lower their earnings expectations do not need to be as high as the smaller entity with the higher cost of capital. It is this relationship to the cost of capital that makes these companies appear to overpay for existing hotels as viewed from the smaller entities' perspective.

By driving up the price of existing hotels, these companies lower the achievable returns of the smaller companies when both are seeking the same types of hotels. This is one reason smaller companies seek out hotels to buy that the larger companies may not pursue for one reason or another.

The smaller company needs to deal with sellers who are patient and wait while the capital for the purchase is raised. The seller will wait because they have been unable to sell it to another buyer or because the price is higher. In either case the return will be lower or the risk is higher for the buyer. After all, why wouldn't anyone else buy the hotel?

In the end, the company with less capital cannot afford to make mistakes and has to maximize cash flow by being a very good hotel marketer and operator. The company with more capital and higher returns can, of course, afford to pay premium wages to its key executives and other staff. The cost and availability of capital affects every aspect of competition in the hotel industry in very fundamental ways.

# 6

# Public Market Financing

In a world where there is a general shortage of capital, hospitality companies must now work much harder in the global competition for money. And as the industry begins to recover in many countries from the excesses of the 1980s, the search is on for new solutions to the capital dilemma.

Accentuating the dilemma is the fad that the losses of the early 1990s and the associated declines in property values have scared away many of the industry's traditional private capital providers. And they do not appear to be returning anytime soon. So it is not surprising that in some markets around the world there is strong interest in public financial markets as a place to seek capital, even though they tend to present some very unique challenges.

Securitization of hotel property and corporate financing has been a popular item in capital markets in the United States during the last several years and looks set to become a permanent feature on the financing landscape. Elsewhere around the world, the use of public markets to fund the international hotel industry is spotty at best. But before visiting some of the new public market frontiers of hospitality industry finance, let us first look at what is going on ix' the United States.

For many years, the U.S. hotel industry benefited from the largesse of private institutional capital, primarily the insurance industry, savings institutions and commercial banks to fund property expansion and acquisition. With these resources no longer as available, the industry has been forced to turn to alternative sources such as the public market and has had to adjust to a new set of rules.

## Real Estate Investment Trusts (REITs)

As 1994 came to a close, Securitization of hotel property and mortgages in the United States was a very hot topic. Real Estate Investment Trusts or REITs (which distribute earnings from real estate, free of corporate taxes) had become high fliers in the stock market. Having finally dealt with the structuring challenges that are unique to REITs and previously made hotel REIT formations problematic, a series of issues came to market in late 1993. These tended to be relatively small issues but they delivered some of the best stock performance in the REIT sector, with investor interest driven largely by the turnaround in the U.S. hotel industry that continues to this day.

Following these initial successes, secondary offerings came to market during 1994 and the general enthusiasm was palpable. But with interest rate escalations throughout the year, the fervor began to fade and by late 1994, the market had retreated. Uncertainty concerning the outlook for hotel REITs was widespread with the conventional wisdom being that it would be a while before we would see any resurgence of interest.

Well, what a difference a year can make. This past year finally turned out to be a significant one for public market financing of the U.S. hotel industry. There was a renewed interest in REITs late in 1995 signalled by the successful launch of the largest hotel REIT yet—the $305 million Patriot American issue involving a portfolio of 20 hotels. And earlier in the year, Starwood Capital successfully recapitalised Hotel Investors Trust, a "grandfathered" REIT that had been operating for years with a unique paired share structure that allows the REIT to manage as well as own property—something other REITs are not allowed to do.

As these large hotel REITs have come to market, there appears to be an appreciation for size that translates into more favourable pricing. This suggests that small capitalization REITs may not see as much popularity as heretofore when they essentially had the market to themselves.

REITs both large and small are but examples, however, in a large public financial marketplace that is increasingly serving the capital needs of the U.S. hotel industry. During the last four years, approximately $4 billion of capital has been raised for publicly traded hotel companies and $1 billion for hotel REITs—split evenly between debt and equity. And the pace quickened in 1995 with a steadily rising stock market. Hotel industry financings were up by one-third over the prior year at approximately $2 billion. Following the fall-off in the REIT market late in 1994, the market for new hotel REITs had been slow in returning. But with the success of the large Patriot American deal, the market seems ready for more.

Interest rates, however, have a big impact on the REIT market, so future activity will be sensitive to interest rate volatility. on the basis of a stable interest environment, however, it is estimated that hotel REITs might represent as much as ~ billion in 19%. Easier to predict than volume is the style or structure of future hotel REIT financings. They are likely to be large and well-covered by Wall Street's research analysts—an essential element if an issue is to gain any respectability and following. Hotel REITs have also tended to be all equity offerings with lines of credit to fund expansion—but these lines can run out quickly following an active property acquisition program.

Future hotel REITs will therefore need to develop capital structures that present blends of debt and equity in an effort to reduce the weighted cost of capital and provide for better balance as the capital base is expanded. Since quality sponsorship is so critical to success in public markets, it also appears likely that we will see fewer Initial Public Offerings and more secondary offerings involving the return to market of well-established hotel companies with a proven track record. No matter how much enthusiasm exists for the industry's positive economic situation, there is little doubt the focus in the future will be on management and its ability to deliver through the next cycle.

### *"C" Corporations*

In addition to the return of hotel REITs last year, there was also a resurgence of activity involving "C" Corporations—traditionally structured companies that have historically been the main players in the public market, A series of new C-corp issues attracted a great deal of institutional investor interest, something that is not always as prevalent on the REIT side of the market. Some small C- corp issues also showed very strong growth stories as the hotel market has turned around. This has attracted a lot of new investors, which is clearly healthy in broadening the base of investor support for the industry.

An interesting trend is the growing acceptance of hotel real estate as part of a public company's balance sheet. Notwithstanding the tendency for the stock market to focus on short-term earnings, some of the recent hotel C corp issues have suggested that hotel property ownership can be appreciated, particularly if it delivers operating leverage in a period of rising occupancy. Of course this appreciation can disappear quickly in a downturn when the leverage works in reverse and delivers losses very quickly.

The public market tends to value a growth story. Working against this concept in the REIT arena is the requirement of the tax code that 95 percent of a REIT's earnings be distributed out to the investors each year. As a consequence, for those companies trying to build franchise value through customer relationships and in need of a constant source of reinvestment capital, the REIT structure is not generally a suitable vehicle. But for those with large real estate portfolios, judicious use of the REIT format for "off balance sheet" property financing can produce a satisfactory outcome.

The lease format used by hotel REITs to address the tax laws' prohibition of involvement in the management of the property, tends to secure a long-term involvement with the property—something that is of particular value in a market where traditional property owner/manager relationships have become far more tenuous and unpredictable. In the context of the hospitality industry at large, it is worth mentioning the gaming industry's involvement with public market financing.

Gaming companies have long been involved with the public markets as a result of not being able to tap into private institutional sources of money. Without the respectability that it has today, gaming companies originally had to operate in the high-yield market. And as the gaming sector grew and the earnings escalated with new jurisdictions, a compelling story for gaming stocks has developed in recent years. More recently we have seen the setbacks of poor press, some negative votes against new jurisdictions and one or two high-profile bankruptcies. This can quickly dampen the enthusiasm, and so it remains to be seen as to what the longer-term public market environment will be like for gaming companies.

For those with experienced management, a well established franchise and customer following, and a position in established jurisdictions, there should be few difficulties. For those at the margin, however, it will be another story. And indeed we can expect to see a consolidation and shakeout as the gaming industry refocuses its attention on the strong players who are well-positioned to benefit from the trends in a variety of gaming jurisdictions across the country.

## Public Market

In evaluating whether to take a hospitality company to the public market for the first time, it is worth reviewing some simple fundamentals to determine if a company has what it takes to make it through the rigorous initial public offering process. Look for the following: the nature and energy level of the management team, stability of earnings, a solid outlook for growth and a focused story and business concept. Other issues to be contended with include the extent of existing leverage, the current owner's objectives and pricing expectations and the need for debt versus equity and their relative costs.

Otherwise successful companies also must recognise that taking a company public for the first time will probably mean facing a discount in value to account for the unknown. The countervailing view is that public market investors driven by the hype surrounding a bull market may value a high-profile hospitality company significantly in excess of what the private market might judge the stock to be worth—the herd mentality one might say. Timing is, of course, everything. As Wall Street becomes more involved in hotel property financing, it is not surprising that the rating agencies (Standard & Poor, Duff & Phelps, Fitch and Moody's) have begun to play a role.

Ratings have tended to be associated with the packaging of small hotel mortgages into Real Estate Mortgage Investment Conduits or "REMICs." Such conduits tranche the capital into various risk levels that carry a range of ratings and are priced accordingly. REMICs were expected to play a big role in hotel financing. especially as these programs were supported by some of the country's largest franchisors as a service to their franchisees. But they turned out to be relatively expensive for borrowers of small amounts. As the industry turned around, there was more competition from local banks willing to finally take a closer look at their neighbourhood borrowers who had been ignored since the real estate collapse in 1991.

As the rating agencies look at hotel debt issues, the factors of importance include portfolio diversification, the adequacy of management fees, the presence of satisfactory replacement reserves and the structure. Whether rating agencies can play a role in encouraging an expanded role for public market financing of the hotel sector remains to be seen. The early signs are that they are interested in understanding the business and appear willing to participate.

And yet even if there is a willingness on the part of the rating agency community to play a role, it must be recognised that at its heart, the public market is far more fickle than the private market. Sentiments of sup port and enthusiasm for an industry can evaporate quickly if there are unexpected setbacks. Conventional wisdom at the moment, however, seems to suggest that the U.S. hotel industry's fundamentals are positive and the upward trend in profitability should continue for at least two more years.

Demand for hotel rooms, however, tracks extremely closely with the underlying change in Gross Domestic Product. So as goes the economy, thus will follow the hotel industry. And if the economy falters, expect to see some major interruption in the otherwise rosy outlook for hotel stocks and debt issues. But even if the industry continues on its present positive track, we should not assume that the public markets will provide all of the answers to the liquidity crisis for the industry. Considering the overall size of hotel financing needs in the United States, which we estimate at $8 billion annually, the public markets account for only a modest portion of the need at approximately 15 percent.

Because of the hotel industry's fragmented structure, its real estate orientation and its general reputation as part real estate/part business, we have not seen as many publicly quoted hotel companies as one might expect in an industry of its size. This hopefully will change in future years as the hospitality industry gains further respectability and hotel corporations enlarged through the process of consolidation seek broader access to public capital. Consolidation can also have a counterpoint, however, and in the U.S. hotel and gaming industries this means de-consolidation. Two companies are of particular note in having split or attempted to split their gaming and hotel operations—Promus and Hilton.

Marriott Corporation split for different reasons in an attempt to separate their real estate from their operational activities. And finally Sheraton Hotels, a stalwart of the U.S. hospitality scene, is now part of a split-up by parent ITT of its varied businesses into three groupings. The first, ITT Destinations, is the consolidation of its hospitality, gaming, sports and entertainment businesses. The public market reactions to these reconstitutions of hospitality companies have by-and-large been favourable, suggesting that it pays to continuously look "outside the organisational box" when trying to create shareholder value.

As hotel groups become larger and operate on a truly global basis, we are likely to see simultaneous hotel company listings in key financial markets around the world such as New York, London and Tokyo. one of the advantages of such international public market exposure relates to the quest that many hospitality companies have for global brand presence. Customer focus deriving from a brand strategy can quite reasonably tie into shareholder relationships on a global scale. It is just a matter of time.

## Financial Markets

Chris Evans, director of corporate finance-hospitality and leisure in the firm's London office, reports that London's public market has not historically been of major significance in the financing of development, or of mergers and acquisition activity in the hospitality and leisure sectors in the United Kingdom.

In the past, many lenders and institutional and individual investors have viewed the hospitality industry somewhat suspiciously, and have preferred to provide corporate debt to hotel companies or to purchase shares in quoted hotel companies to spread sector risk as widely as possible. This preference has meant that the industry has been characterised by relatively unsophisticated financings.

The ownership structure of the industry in the United Kingdom has also been of influence in this regard. Hotels tend to be owner-operated and, with relatively few exceptions, the major hotel owning and operating companies are subsidiaries of conglomerates. Where capital has been required for development and M&A activity at such companies, it has normally been provided by the parent company since, generally speaking, corporate debt at such a level is rather less expensive than project or deal-specific debt.

Furthermore, in the United Kingdom there are relatively few independent hotel management companies operating hotels under franchises from the major international brands. In the United States such independent companies have been great users of public market capital. Those which do exist in the United Kingdom are small—in most instances operating two or three hotels. Development and acquisitions activity at such companies tend to be financed on a project-by-project basis with security provided by the asset to be financed plus, in many cases, additional company or personal guarantees.

The one major exception to this general rule is the Whitbread Hotel Group (formerly Scott's Hotels), which owns and operates 13 hotels under franchise agreements with Marriott International. Whitbread Hotels Group, however, is a relatively small subsidiary of Whitbread PLC the brewing company, and funds for the £185 million acquisition of the 13 Scott's hotels were provided by the parent company. Special share issues (such as rights issues and convertible preference share issues), however, have been used among the relatively few quoted "pure" hotel companies—particularly during the late 198Os. Oueen's Moat Houses financed a series of corporate and individual hotel property acquisitions via rights issues.

Turning to the future in the United Kingdom, given the capital intensive nature of the industry, we have observed an increasing interest among both the major conglomerates and the (few) independent hotel owned management companies in innovative financing methods—particularly in off-balance sheet financing. We believe that this interest will extend in the future to public capital markets. As recovery in the sector in the U.K. continues apace, we foresee a much wider interest among both providers and users of such capital.

From Tokyo, Arthur Andersen partner Kenji Ushitora reports that with the Japanese economy struggling for a soft landing and with banks still trying to deal with the challenges posed by their sizable exposure to real estate, the hospitality industry does not maintain any particular visibility in the public markets. The hospitality sector has been traditionally housed in large corporations with financing obscured from public view.

And in Germany, the hospitality industry s experience with the public markets is in its developmental stages, reports Hospitality Consulting Director John Litzenberger of Arthur Andersen's Frankfurt office. Kempinski is the only publicly quoted company with just six hotels in Germany and a total portfolio of only 30 properties. With an overbuilt domestic market, there is little demand for new capital, public or otherwise to fund new activities.

The large German chains are by-and-large privately owned — Maritim, Steigenberger and Arabella — and do not come to the public market for capital. Closed-end property funds that do trade publicly will have some exposure to hotel real estate but it tends to be mixed into a large diversified portfolio. The German hospitality sector clearly is a long way from using public market financing in the way that companies do in the United States. This might change in the future, suggests Litzenberger, but it will be a long rime in the making.

In Australia, Phil Kasselis, Director of Hospitality Consulting in the firm's Sydney office, reports that the Australian Stock Exchange has 16 listed companies in a Tourism and Leisure Index. The TL Index was established in 1994 with over half the index made up of casino stocks. The index outperformed the market by a factor of 3:1 in 1995, confirming the enthusiasm investors have for the fast developing gaming industry and the fundamentals of the hotel sector, where demand growth continues to outstrip supply and should continue to do so for the next several years and probably up to the year 2000 when Sydney hosts the Olympics.

In the Australian property funds, where hotels as an asset class are generally under-represented, we should see an increase in the allocation of capital to this sector as profits return and the hotel industry outlook remains positive. Casino operators, hotel owners and hotel management companies will also expand their presence in the public financial markets, finding it a cheaper and easier way to raise capital than traditional bank debt. Large institutions are also likely to increase their involvement with publicly listed hospitality companies.

The international hotel industry has a long way to go in truly capitalising on the opportunities afforded by public financial markets. The securitization of real estate has developed rapidly in recent years in the United States, but may be much longer in coming to other markets elsewhere, where traditional methods of financing are slow to change. Financial adversity will, however, force users of capital to source their needs in the public domain. It will require some big adjustments in approach and some serious corporate soul searching to get there. But it can be worth it and in a world of capital shortage, hospitality companies may have no choice but to force their way in. And as they say in the travel business... getting there is half the fun.

## Debt Financing and Ownership of Lodging Industry

Since 1990 the financing and ownership of lodging real estate have undergone substantial transformations. Specifically, the owner's equity, required for hotel real-estate deals has fundamentally changed the way lodging assets and companies are financed. Hotel buyers, developers, owners, and managers need to understand the different alternatives to securing debt, as well as the viability of numerous financing strategies—an intimidating task in increasingly volatile markets.

One of the issues in lodging finance is the ratio of debt to equity. Debt can be beneficial, of course, but only up to a point—beyond which the costs of potential financial distress begin to outweigh the benefits of leverage. That is an important issue for investors because debt-to-invested capital affects a hotel's cost of capital and, therefore, the overall value of the property. The lodging industry has earned a reputation as a high-risk business for lenders and mortgage investors. Obtaining financing for a lodging property calls for creativity, tenacity, and flexibility.

Today, hotel developers and operators find themselves not only aggressively competing for a constantly changing pool of funds (both equity and debt), but also having to deal with increasingly complex terms and conditions for the efficient use of those funds. Before pursuing debt-financing alternatives hotel investors need first to consider four basic elements, namely

(1) business risk,

(2) the need for financial flexibility,

(3) the degree of management's risk aversion, and

(4) tax considerations.

*Business risk*: Business risk is inherent in the property, and is related to the volatility of its sales and its degree of operating leverage. In most cases, hotels can compensate for a large amount of business risk by employing a relatively conservative capital structure.

*The need for financial flexibility*: The fact that interest must be paid on debt (but dividends do not have to be paid on equity) has important implications for hotels that want as much financial flexibility as possible. The debt–equity ratio can be affected by the extent to which suppliers of debt capital fail to assess the risk of financial distress accurately.

*The degree of ownership's risk aversion*: Hotel owners have to be comfortable with the risk that they are taking.

If management has a great aversion to taking risk, it will seek to use a conservative amount of debt. This is one that gives the property the maximum amount of financial flexibility and imposes the least amount of leverage. Aggressive owners, on the other hand, may be willing to incur risk inherent by employing a large amount of debt in the capital structure precisely because of the leverage it gives to the bottom line.

*Tax considerations*: Tax considerations include the marginal tax rate of the ownership entity, and the way the tax law treats payments to various suppliers of investment capital. For example, the fact that interest on debt capital is tax deductible, while dividends paid to suppliers of preferred or common equity capital are not, can influence the targeted debt levels. Generally, the higher the marginal tax rate is, the greater the incentive to use more debt.

### *Real-estate Capital-flows*

The level of capital flows to real estate between 1983 and 2001 highlights the importance of private debt in the marketplace, which is expected to continue to play a significant role in future capital funding. Capital flows are anticipated to return to a temperate level in 2002, as lenders and investors re-enter the market. In fact, total capital flows to real estate in 2002 are predicted to increase by 12.5 percent over 2001, driven primarily by the private market.

Between 1983 and 2001 lodging-industry senior-mortgage commitments fluctuated considerably, slumping in 1991 at only $160 million and peaking in 1986 at approximately $1.8 billion. In general, when the prime lending rate declines, senior-mortgage commitments tend to increase in an inverse correlation. According to the American Council of Life Insurers (ACLI), in 2001 a cumulative total of approximately $7.4 billion in commercial mortgages held by insurance companies was secured by hotel and motel properties, compared to $6.3 billion in 2000, indicating the continuing reliance on debt in the lodging industry. As a point of reference, in 2001 the lodging sector constituted 4.3 percent of total senior-mortgage commitments.

The hotel-debt capital markets are currently characterised by high volatility, although interest rates are low, including the prime lending rate (Exhibit 4). However, there is still interest in established properties operating in markets with high barriers to entry, such as New York, Chicago, and San Francisco. The spread between the London Interbank Offer Rate (LIBOR) and the prime lending rate is essentially the profit to the lender.

## Fundamentals of Hotel Debt-financing

The cheapest additional capital to raise is debt capital, so debt should be the first source of new capital. Only when a hotel company has raised so much debt that its financial flexibility is becoming impaired, or its cost of debt becomes too high, should it consider raising more funds by selling shares of common stock or even lodging assets.

Although there are multiple reasons why the possibility of debt financing increases the value of hotel real estate, this does not imply that borrowing $65 million on a $100 million hotel automatically increases the value of the property. If it did, then all investors would acquire properties using leverage. So, there is more to leverage than meets the eye, especially due to operational issues.

The potential benefits of debt are usually already factored into the market value of the property, so that the hotel's value is usually independent of specific financing decisions. Naturally, a 7-percent long-term loan in a 9-

percent market does add value, but that value is derived from below-market financing and not from the decision to acquire debt per se.

When a hotel owner uses debt, the interest payments are tax deductible. Furthermore, the use of debt increases the tax basis beyond the equity investment, thus enhancing the tax shelter generated from depreciation. Those two tax-related fundamentals allow the hotel owner who uses debt to reduce the IRS's share of net operating income.

The most obvious use of debt financing is the reduction of the minimum investment necessary in any given hotel deal. Because investors generally have limited capital resources, a reduced minimum investment in one transaction allows them to spread their wealth over several investments.

As diversification reduces portfolio risk, then lower risk should translate into higher value. Combining financing possibilities with various forms of ownership, the decision maker can create new risk-return opportunities—meaning that new investments fit specific investor needs. As such, the flexibility to tailor the investment to suit the hotel owner is an additional benefit of using debt financing.

### *Advantages and Disadvantages of Debt Financing*

The decision to use leverage should be made in the context of uncertain asset returns and the portfolio implications of the leverage decision. The great advantage of hotel debt financing at both the property and portfolio level is maximising the return on equity, while a chief disadvantage is stifling management's energy and creativity. Other advantages and disadvantages are shown below.

*At the Property Level*

*Advantages*

— The use of leverage in hotel real-estate investing is a way to maximise the return on equity through a relatively small down payment. When building real estate, leverage helps one grow fast without extreme risk. The best scenario is when property values increase faster than the interest charged on borrowed funds.

— A debt load is an incentive that forces a hotel's management to maintain efficiency, since the financial leverage will work against earnings if management becomes lax and permits net operating income to decline.

— Debt increases the interest tax shield, which increases the cash flow to equity, and should enhance the value of the property.

— Leverage uses other entities' capital while allowing maximum control over the business.

— Debt is an "enabling tool" that allows investors to tap into potential equity that would otherwise be unattainable.

— With an increasing property value, the initial debt can significantly increase equity levels upon disposition.

*Disadvantages*

— High debt levels impose potential costs on a property in the form of the risk of default and the loss of financial flexibility.

— Leveraging can, in some cases, "enslave" a hotel to the lender, and stifle management's creativity and energy.

*At the Portfolio Level*

*Advantages*

— Non-recourse mortgage debt provides the borrower with a "put (sell) option." That is, should the values of the properties fall beneath the loan balance, the investor may elect to hand back the hotels by tendering a deed for the properties to the lender in satisfaction of the indebtedness.

— The use of mortgage debt increases the diversification possibilities within the real-estate portfolio.

— In pension fund management, mortgage debt can be used for greater alignment between the "duration" of the investor's assets and liabilities. Duration is a concept designed to measure the sensitivity of assets and liabilities to a change in the level of interest rates. One of the goals of pension fund management is to match the duration of the pension's retirement liabilities with assets of identical duration.

  In this way, the pension fund's surplus is considered to be "immunised", such that a change in the value of the pension fund's liabilities caused by a change in interest rates is completely offset by a change in the value of the pension fund's assets. An investor can use mortgage financing to alter the duration of the leveraged real estate investment. Essentially, the duration of fixed-rate mortgage debt offsets the asset's duration.

*Disadvantages*

— Financing real estate with debt is equivalent to "shorting" a portion of the investor's fixed-income portfolio, and therefore alters the investor's portfolio allocations.

— An increased equity-yield fallacy is possible when investors focus on the leveraged yield rather than on the asset return in making their purchase decisions.

— Long-term debt tends to lower the weighted average cost of capital (WACC, or discount rate) because of the tax-deductibility of interest. However, the introduction of large quantities of debt into a portfolio's capital structure can result in higher levels of financial risk, which cause the WACC to rise.

Leverage makes the volatility of investor returns greater than the volatility of the value of the underlying property. In other words, if the return on the hotel asset itself (before financing costs and taxes) exceeds the pre-tax cost of the mortgage debt used to finance the property, leverage is positive and the pre-tax return on the investor's equity in the hotel will be greater than the pre-tax return on the asset itself. However, if the pre-tax return on the hotel asset is less than the cost of financing the investment, leverage is negative, and the return on the investor's equity that is invested in the hotel will be less than the pre-tax return on the asset itself.

To demonstrate this basic principle, suppose that a full-service urban hotel is acquired for $30,000,000 and the revenues and total expenses are $10,000,000 and $7,000,000, respectively. Exhibit 6 shows the investor's return on equity if the hotel is purchased with no debt (unleveraged), and if it is 70-percent financed with a 7.5-percent, 25-year amortization, monthly payment conventional loan (ignoring the effect of depreciation and income taxes).

The leverage is positive because the return on the hotel (10 percent) is greater than the cost of debt (7.5 percent), so that the leveraged return on equity (15.8 percent) is greater than the unleveraged return on the asset (10 percent). Although the return on equity increases with 70-percent leverage, this increase is accompanied by higher risk exposure to the investor's equity position. Therefore, the resulting return on equity derived from the amount of debt used needs to be constantly measured against the investor's required return on equity and tolerance level for risk exposure. The factor that is most important in producing leverage is the amount of debt used to finance the acquisition of the hotel, rather than the interest rate on that debt.

### *Sources of Debt Financing*

In general there are four sources for third-party financing available via the debt-capital markets. These are: bank financing (domestic and overseas), insurance companies, conduit-loan securitization, and single-asset securitization. More specifically, Exhibit 8 focuses on typical loan terms and motivations by source of debt financing.

### *Mezzanine Financing*

Mezzanine loans have filled the void in lodging-industry financing before, specifically in the early and mid 1990s when real-estate markets put some loan institutions in jeopardy through defaults. Banks, in turn, began to finance less of the construction costs with the first mortgage. The need for gap financing has recently re-emerged because public markets have been skeptical of the industry's expansion. Mezzanine funding has become an attractive finance option for hotel owners being faced with a "credit squeeze." The comparative advantages of mezzanine financing are demonstrated via a simplified numeric benchmark of the structure.

On the assumption that a hotel valued at $20 million was earning a net operating income of $2.4 million a year and achieved annual NOI growth of 3 percent, Exhibit 10 shows the difference in return for a hotel owner between a traditional and a mezzanine debt structure over a six-year period. Because of the leveraged nature of mezzanine finance, the internal rate of return would be sensitive to any changes in NOI.

### *Fundamentals of Hotel-debt Refinancing*

In today's jittery capital markets, and apart from private equity and entrepreneurial sources, there is still financing available for strong properties with strong sponsorship. For the most part, lenders are not usually concerned about the spreads and lower interest rates. Rather, what sparks the deal-making process is basically whether the deal shapes up as a strong one or not. Nonetheless, with the current low interest rates, there should be some straight refinancings occurring, provided that the underlying assets can support the deal.

While lenders are still hesitant to fund hotel loans, some are beginning to evaluate their current stance, especially as the lodging sector's worst is behind it. Whereas hotel fundamentals are not yet where they were before September 11, they are well on their way towards improvement. Therefore, a lender underwriting a loan using a property's existing financials would have a solid mortgage a few months hence, when the market improves even further.

An example of a high-profile refinancing deal involves the Chicago Marriott Downtown. The owners of the Marriott Downtown, a 1,192-room hotel, have recently begun shopping for $120 million of refinancing for the upscale asset. The Carlyle Group and LaSalle Hotel Properties (the real estate investment trust) bought the property in early 2000 for $175 million, or nearly $150,000 per key, from a venture between John Buck Company and the Morgan Stanley Real Estate Fund.

The acquisition was financed with a $120 million floating-rate mortgage that was provided by GE Capital and the Bank of Montreal. The search for a new mortgage is being prompted by the fact that the existing mortgage comes due in about eight months. It is not known, however, whether that mortgage can be extended, and if it can, to what level its interest rate would climb. The loan carries a rate pegged to LIBOR plus 275 basis points, which translated to 4.9 percent at the end of 2001.

*Debt Restructurings*

During the period 2001–2002 quite a few hotel owners have not been able to meet their debt payments. This has caused a number of companies and properties to consider restructuring their debts. Some of those hotels may be able to resolve their situation with their creditors, in what is known as a "workout," without resorting to court proceedings.

Debt restructurings can enable a company to survive if key components are kept in focus. For example, the debtor must realise that timing is paramount. If a hotel company waits until it cannot cover payroll, it is probably too late for anyone else to provide assistance, implying that reorganisation efforts need to commence as soon as possible. In addition, a company must address any balance-sheet issues fairly quickly. These normally include long-term debt (mortgages); short-term debt (lines of credit); trade debt (debt owed to food vendors); and employee claims (insurance).

Balance-sheet issues can be addressed by projecting the amount of cash that will be available to repay creditors, and by constructing a repayment plan that will fit those projections. However, if the projections bring to light that the company is better off liquidating than continuing operations, then the company may have a legal obligation to cease operating and liquidate for the benefit of its creditors.

Debt restructuring really means creative financing. Becoming creative tends to become necessary when a hotel is unable to produce the cash flow required to cover an owner's debt service. Quite often, creative financing is also applied to assist owners in accepting substantial equity losses at the point of sale and to move on. In either event, the lender-owner takes a hit on his or her capital or suffers lower-than-market-rate yields as a result of the debt restructuring.

Restructuring primarily involves selling businesses, renegotiating loans, and raising additional capital. Warren Buffet's mid-2001 bailout of troubled commercial real-estate lender Finova involved the reorganisation of more than $10 billion of debt, the majority of which were bad loans. The term "hotel debt restructuring" refers to general reformation cases, as well as to troubled-debt restructuring.

General-debt restructuring simply refers to debt reformation whereby the lender has incurred no losses from the restructuring of debt. That is, where creditors have granted concessions by reducing the interest rate:

(i) to reflect changes in market fundamentals;

(ii) to maintain the relationship with the debtor;

(iii) by extending the repayment period, or

(iv) granting a grace period.

During the grace period the debtor continues to pay interest only at the original contractual interest rate where the creditors' analyses have shown that the debtor is able to repay the full amount of the loan (principal and interest) as agreed in the original loan contract. On the other hand, troubled-debt restructuring refers to cases where financial institutions incur losses from the restructuring due to one or a combination of the following variables.

— Reduction of the principal or accrued interest.

- — Loss from restructuring through acceptance of a transfer of assets in debt repayment where fair value of assets is lower than the credit written off.
- — Concessions in the terms of loan repayment resulting in a fall in the present value of cash flows such that this value is lower than the sum of book value of the credits outstanding and the accrued interest.
- — Loss from the debt-restructuring calculations based on the market value of the debtor's business, the fair value of the collateral asset, or loss from other techniques in debt restructuring, such as from debt-to-equity swaps.

Debt restructuring should be carried out to maximise the creditor's chances of getting repayment subject to the debtor's ability to repay the loan, or in some other way improve on the conditions set out in the parties' original contract. In particular, hotel-debt restructuring should be carried out to help debtors who have difficulties repaying a loan due to adverse market conditions or property-level mismanagement, but are expected to recover in the future.

The lender will ensure that restructuring is not carried out with the objective of postponing or avoiding debt classification or provisioning requirements, or the avoidance of stopping interest accruals. Distressed-debt investors who buy into restructuring processes have several advantages. Since they, along with their capital-markets advisor, are controlling the negotiations, they are protected to an extent from external-market conditions. They are also in control when restructured debt is returned to the market, which is when its full potential value will be realised. However, the challenge is to anticipate correctly the time and difficulty likely to be involved in a restructuring. The real test of a successful restructuring is the ability for the market to pick up on the residual package, whether it is debt or hybrid or equity, and trade it.

Financial institutions can contract an independent party such as a specialised group of experienced hotel-debt restructuring strategists. Hotel real-estate investment banks can establish a formal strategy for debt restructuring, whereby the highest level of management should participate directly in formulating this strategy.

The degree of creativity necessary to allow a hotel business to be financially independent often depends on fiscal pressures pressing down on either the debtor or creditor. For instance, a bank that has written down a hotel loan and taken back the property will be able to accept a market-level price for it, but may demand "concessions" to provide financing. On the other hand, a brittle seller owning a hotel that has not fulfilled the debt obligations to the lender may be in no position to negotiate. He or she may have to accept a soft note with minimal payments if the equity in the property is insecure. In both instances, a sale is contemplated.

Characteristically, the first two or three years after a sale or restructuring allow for a "breather" period and for conservative debt-service levels, often at below-market rates. Occasionally, the difference between the cash-payment debt schedule and a market interest rate is accrued and stapled on to the principal amount of the loan. The due date of the accrual, while negotiable, is normally deferred until the loan matures. After the breather period, the creditor may expect an interest-rate incentive (kicker) in consideration of his or her earlier patience.

For example, the creatively recast debt might bear an 8.5-percent base interest rate with additional interest equal to a percentage of gross room sales. Conceptually, that implies that when the business improves, the creditor is expected to share in the upside. In addition to this bonus-payment plan, or instead of it, the creditor (or the advisor) may negotiate to receive a percentage of the hotel's future resale price. This often falls in the 25-percent range, and can be a helpful inducement to convince a creditor to be patient today. A clear definition of how this future bonus is paid and calculated is important to avoid future problems.

# 7

# Managing Hotel Investments

During the past several years the hotel industry has grown from being one of the worst to one of the top performing investment asset classes. And during this same time the strong investment performance of hotels has attracted substantial investment capital. More recently returns have levelled off for most hotels and have actually declined for many types of hotel investments. And as a result the industry is already experiencing the contraction of investment capital.

The on-going availability of investment capital can be expected to ultimately be closely linked to investment return performance (in particular relative to the risk and returns of alternative investments). And accordingly, one of the major challenges of the industry going forward will be maintaining hotel investment returns at levels adequate to continue to attract investment capital.

## Investment Performance Barometers

The information available on investment performance for the hospitality industry historically has been very limited. For several years the industry has tracked the numerator (or overall "profit" or cash flow generated by hotels) but has been unable to relate this number to a denominator (or the total dollars invested in hotels) at a given point in time. Also in the past the industry has not been able to isolate the capital appreciation versus income return components for hotels nor to develop a total investment return performance barometer/indices for the industry.

In response to the need for better industry investment return performance data, the American Hotel & Motel Association's Industry Real Estate Financial Advisory Council, in conjunction with Cornell University, developed the "Lodging Property Index". The index, initially published in 1996, represents the first of its kind in the hotel industry.

While the index represents a great leap forward in the compilation of return on investment performance numbers for hotels, the information available for the industry as a whole is still very limited. Going forward the industry will need to focus on expanding the return on investment performance data available for the industry as a whole to provide a more reliable barometer for investors to evaluate hotel investment performance.

### *Financial Performance Monitoring & Analysis*

With advances in technology, there is a tremendous amount of information (financial and sales and marketing in particular) available for review and analysis. On the one hand the voluminous information available can be very helpful for better understanding and diagnosing problems as well as for identifying areas for improving performance. Unfortunately, on the other, the amount of information potentially available to be reviewed and analysed can be very overwhelming.

One of the major challenges in the future will be to streamline reporting to both facilitate comprehension as well as to potentially bridge the tremendous communication gaps (between investor and operational reporting; between asset and property managers; between corporate and on-site management and even among executive committee members) emerging.

*Shareholder and Investor Reporting*

The information in many shareholder and investor reports, for REIT's in particular, is currently presented at a very high level of aggregation making it very difficult and in some instances virtually impossible to really understand what is going on on an individual property basis. Additionally, in some instances critical information even at the portfolio level, let alone at the individual property level, has been missing in public offering and/or shareholder reports.

*Back to Basics*

With the tremendous emphasis in recent years on the deal making or transaction side of the business as an industry we have lost focus on the customer, the employee and the underlying business fundamentals of operating hotels.

— *The customer* - recent surveys indicate that hotel customer satisfaction is at an all time low.

— *The employee* - employee turnover for the industry as a whole is also at an all time high.

— *Underlying Business Fundamentals* - there continue to be substantial opportunities for many hotels to improve both revenue and expense performance. For many hotels there are untapped revenue and yield management opportunities. And on the expense side, promotion and distribution costs and labour management represent areas for further improving performance.

— *Going forward we can anticipate a return to the basics* — a renewed focus on the customer, the employee and the management of revenue and expenses.

### *Technology Issues*

There are several technology issues that can be expected to represent on-going challenges for hotel owners/asset managers in the future. First is the basic challenge of staying informed! Technology currently represents one of the largest capital investment areas. To make informed decisions it is critical that owners/asset managers understand a hotels basic technology needs and the cost versus benefits of alternative approaches to addressing them.

We can anticipate that the issues of the ownership of data along with other proprietary as well as interface issues will continue to evolve as potential major areas of concern. And increasingly we are seeing challenges...particularly in the area of yield management...in bridging the automated versus cognitive or learning application perspectives in technology.

### *Managing Potential Conflicts of Interest*

While historically conflicts of interest have focused primarily on third party management and/or franchise issues, more recently we have seen conflicts of interest develop in other areas. With the significant changes in the forms of ownership of hotels experienced in the past few years, we are seeing potential conflicts emerge in certain investment structures.

Additionally, with advances in technology along with the significant increase in merger and acquisitions activity in recent years, new areas of potential conflicts have also emerged that will need to be addressed in the future. In the area of technology, the issues of proprietary systems and the ownership of data can be expected to present challenges and possible conflicts between an owner/investor and a third party chain and/or franchisor's interests. And with the substantial recent merger and acquisitions activity, potential conflicts of interest are emerging—in the sales and marketing area in particular.

### *Management Contracts*

Going forward we can anticipate that owners/investors will place much greater emphasis on managing third party operator/manager risk and exposure issues. Delegations of authority and control, indemnifications, default and termination provisions etc. will be expanded and further defined to provide for better alignment of operator accountability with delegations of authority and control and to better address potential conflicts of interest.

We can also anticipate that greater focus will be placed on managing transition and exit strategy issues and concerns. Quite simply, if a major problem and/or conflict cf interest develops an owner needs the ability to timely resolve it—or if it cannot be resolved (which is potentially the case with certain inherent conflicts of interest that are emerging) the ability to reasonably terminate the contract.

And as part of better managing transition exposure in the future, the issues of the ownership of books and records, proprietary computer systems, interim reservations system support, employee rights obligations and responsibilities, the handling of business on the books, the managing of public relations exposure etc.—all need to be addressed up front to mitigate what can be tremendous exposure for a hotel owner if for whatever reason a change in management is necessary.

### *Franchise Contracts*

Shorter term contracts, improved alignment of interests (of franchisor and franchisee), greater focus on direct sales (versus mass advertising and promotion strategies), more potential ala carte value added offerings versus mandatory program requirements—are all areas that we can anticipate the industry will focus on in the future. Additionally, the internet—and the marketing and distribution alternatives it can provide— can be expected to potentially greatly level the playing field between franchisors and franchisees for certain types of hotels.

### *Capital Asset Preservation*

Historically, the hotel industry has lagged far behind other industries in managing the physical assets underlying a hotel investment. There is tremendous untapped potential to improve hotel investment performance via mitigating capital reinvestment exposure through improved preventative maintenance programs and improved capital investment decision making. Going forward we can anticipate that much greater emphasis will be placed both on better preserving capital assets as well as improving up front decision making when initially purchasing capital items.

### *Human Resource Management*

With the tremendous focus in recent years on the transaction side of the business, the industry has lost substantial focus on one of the most critical components of a hotel investment...namely the employee. The hotel business is first and foremost a people business. Neither the most glamorous of hotels nor the most sophisticated or creative financial transactions can insure success in the hotel industry. But rather it is consistently the employees—well trained and motivated employees—that ultimately make the difference in a hotel investment. Human resource management issues—from recruiting, training and motivating employees to managing turnover and labour costs—can be expected to represent huge challenges in the future. Going forward addressing these same issues is not only the right thing to do but represents one of, if not the single greatest opportunity, for improving investment performance.

### Top Ten Investment Challenges Facing the Lodging Industry

1. Finding first mortgage debt capital at loan-to-value ratios and interest rates conducive to achieving targeted equity rates of return.
2. Locating suitable, quality product at a viable price for acquisition and/or rehabilitation by narrowing the bid and ask prices between buyers and sellers.
3. Predicting and quantifying the timing of the hotel industry's rebound for specific lodging markets.
4. Assessing and responding to the long-term impact of the recent recession and 9/11-related revenue and profit declines.
5. Resolving problems being encountered by lenders and borrower with ambiguities and restrictions in conduit loans, REMIC rules and related pooling and servicing agreements.
6. Accessing capital for renovations in light of profitability declines and tighter lending criteria.
7. Credibly and reliably underwriting hotel deals in the current uncertain market.
8. Determining the most reliable cash flow basis to determine appropriate asset pricing strategies to consummate successful deals.
9. Maintaining profit margins in the face of revenue declines and upward salary and wage pressures
10. Coping with the medium- and long-term impact on asset values and product quality from the use of reserves to meet short-term operating needs.

## Development of Hotel Investment Market

ATLANTA, GA., March 16, 2007 – Sound industry fundamentals continued to drive U.S. hotel transaction market activity in 2006. Not only did the one-off and portfolio sales continue to occur thanks to an avalanche of money from private equity funds, some well-known public companies, such as Four Seasons and La Quinta, changed jerseys in response to "can't refuse" offers from previously unfamiliar names in the hotel industry. These observations come from an analysis of data collected in connection with the recently released 2007 edition of Hospitality Investment Survey published by PKF Hospitality Research (PKF-HR), an affiliate of PKF Consulting.

"The lingering question on investors' minds is how to maximise yield in a capital-induced frenzy that continues in the face of lowered revenue growth expectations, increasing upward pressure on operating costs, and questionable exit expectations further out on the investment horizon," said Scott Smith MAI, vice president in the Atlanta office of PKF Consulting. "Historically, market expansions abruptly concluded with recession and either war, catastrophic event, or both. With no clear signs of a recession brewing and considering the unpredictability of catastrophic events, the most likely reason why hotel ADRs and asset prices will come down is supply expansion."

The 2007 edition of Hospitality Investment Survey reflects the cautious optimism of both debt and equity capital providers. With overall capitalisation rates and discount rates near historic lows for this survey, property value increases may be moderating. Yet, cash flow growth keeps investors optimistic. Especially noteworthy among the survey results is the almost two-year increase in the investment holding period. This increase indicates an inclination to view hotels as longer-term "dividend plays" and not so much as short-term opportunistic investments.

Capitalisation rates have received a great deal of attention during this cycle, with prices at or near all-time highs. In 2005, the average capitalisation rate for all hotels reached an all-time low of 8.88 percent. In the 2006 survey, that number edged up 25 basis points to 9.13 percent, indicating that prices are beginning to moderate. Investment grade assets continue to be the most highly sought after with cap rates ranging from 6 to 8 percent in 2006.

Discount rates, or un-leveraged IRRs, for hotels moved down to 12.96 percent. Consequently, the huge 5.5 percent spread last year between the overall capitalisation rate and the discount rate shrunk to 3.83 percent with this survey. The finding suggests that while owner expectations for long-term growth in net operating income have moderated, owners believe the growth rate will continue to exceed the expected rate of inflation.

"Due to the lateness of the cycle, buyers of hotels in 2007 and 2008 should plan on longer holding periods and be willing to give up IRR points due to an absence of meaningful appreciation. The near-term probability of an uptick in capitalisation rates is much higher at this juncture than a downtick. The IRR points given up in appreciation can be gained back, plus some, by running successful dividend plays. Logical investment strategies going forward involve development, where feasible, and when investors can stomach the risk, and efficiently operating what you acquire to maximise NOI," Smith noted.

Despite fears of rising interest rates and Federal Reserve actions, the cost of financing continues to fall. The interest rate for hotel loans stands at less than 7 percent for the first time since this survey began in 1988. Loan-to-value ratios remained slightly below 70 percent, but are above levels in several prior periods. These mortgage terms indicate that

(1) lenders feel adequately protected from a reöccurrence of delinquency and default risk experienced earlier in the 2000s, and

(2) any fears today of overly aggressive hotel underwriting standards are unfounded.

While a buy and hold investment strategy explicitly means not selling anytime soon, implicitly it means holding on to your money. "Hotel economics 101 tells us that ADR growth dominates RevPAR growth after occupancy has reached a threshold where fewer additional guests will be chewing up expenses and hopefully all guests will pay higher room rates," said John B. (Jack) Corgel Ph.D., Senior Advisor to PKF Hospitality Research and the Robert C. Baker Professor of Real Estate, Cornell University School of Hotel Administration.

However, ADR-driven revenues need to be bolstered by either higher service levels and/or better amenities. During past expansions, money was spent elevating service levels and amenity offerings under the assumption that higher paying guests demand such increases. In addition, some money needs to be spent to remain competitive and conform to franchise requirements. But modest renovation projects divert current cash flow from investor coffers. "In this kind of environment, where returns are highly dependent on operating revenues, investors need to carefully evaluate and selectively invest in those projects that promise adequate returns," Corgel concluded.

Hospitality Investment Survey discusses the possibility of unexpected hotel development putting an end to the industry's strong performance measurements. The hotel construction pipeline is full of planned and proposed projects. However, the high cost of construction has kept most of these projects from actually breaking ground.

"If construction costs continue to grow at rates exceeding inflation and property value increases, it is reasonable to assume that existing hotels will be virtual money-printing machines over the next few years. Investors should have great difficulty matching the dividend return on hotels compared to other property types," Corgel observed. "On the other hand, should construction costs decline by 5 to 10 percent, the potential exists for the supply growth to exceed demand growth during the next two years."

"Because of the large number of hotel projects in the proposed and planning stages, and the speed with which projects can move through the pipeline once they become feasible, and due to the presumed sensitivity of supply change to construction cost movements, we recommend that investors closely watch how the prices of land, labour, and materials behave," Corgel advised.

The 2007 Hospitality Investment Survey presents the results from surveys of active hotel owners, equity investors, and debt providers concerning the criteria used for hotel transactions that have, or will, occur during the year. The eight-page report contains tables that show the current and historical averages of a dozen critical investment measurements, including capitalisation rates and mortgage terms. Data are broken out for 10 different property types.

## Political Risk and Foreign Investment Decision

The growing importance and necessity of foreign investment for strengthening economic stability and quickly evolving towards a developed economy in developing countries has generated interest in foreign investment decisions of multinational corporations. Factors which prompt MNCs to enter individual countries have been reported by many studies in a variety of ways. It is also clear that the level of hotel investment is not homogeneous, some countries have significantly more development than others.

For instance, "across the Americas in 1998 the travel and tourism industry will have generated US$ 1.2 trillion in GDP and 33.7 million jobs". But some 70% of new hotel development in Latin America is concentrated in two countries. Brazil in the next few years is expected to have 25,000 new rooms and Mexico 12,000, with Accor, Choice, Sol Melia, Holiday Inn and Hilton being the key international players.

The findings of previous empirical studies show that MNCs consider the political risk of the host country as one of the most important determinants in investment decision making. Such concern is due to the belief that unpredictability and volatility in the political environment of the host market increases the perceived risk and uncertainty experienced by the firm. In turn, this disinclines firms from entering with heavy resource commitments.

### *Political Risk and Instability*

Several scholars claimed there is no single universally accepted definition of political risk. It is most commonly conceived in terms of (usually host) government interference with business operation. Very simply, 'political risk' refers to the possibility that political decisions or events in a country will affect the business climate in such a way that investors will lose money or not make as much money as they expected when the investment was made.

The existing definitions of political risk focus on the concept of political risk from two different perspectives. One group views political risk in terms of governmental or sovereign interference actions. This concept, which is related to all undesired outcomes of political activities of the host government with private businesses, is represented by confiscation, currency repatriation, limits to business transactions and so on. The second group identifies political risk as occurrences of any political events imposed upon the firm. The examples are violence, terrorism, and guerrilla groups.

In the process of defining political risk it is useful to distinguish it from political instability. Carbon argued that instability is a feature of the general environment, whereas risk is something narrower in focus which directly affects the MEN. In other words, political instability, for example, by an unexpected change in government leadership, may not involve political risk for international business. Furthermore, Lewis claimed that political stability in itself is not a sufficient guarantee to tourism or any other kind of industry, especially in the absence of favourable economic conditions.

Political risk is also defined more precisely. Schmidt defines political risk as "the application of host government policies that constrain the business operations of a given foreign investment". He subdivides risk into three main categories: "transfer risk", concerning risk to capital payments; "operational risk", with threats over local source or content; and "ownership control risk", highlighting possibilities of expropriation or confiscation.

Moreover, according to Kennedy political risk can be defined as the risk of a strategic, financial, or personnel loss for a firm because of such non-market factors as macroeconomics and social policies (fiscal, monetary, trade, investment, industrial, income, labour, and development), or events related to political instability (terrorism, riots, coups, civil war, and insurrection). These two types of non-market factors can be called legal - governmental and extra legal political risks. Legal - governmental risks are caused by events that are considered illegitimate by the existing political system.

The difficulty in finding a proper and commonly accepted definition of political risk has presumably prevented many researchers from contributing to this issue and it is also troublesome for building a solid model easily applicable. Furthermore, the scope of political risk may be another deterrent for the development of research in this field.

The growing amount of resource commitment assigned to foreign investment by the increasing number of MNCs has generated particular interest in assessing the relationship between the foreign investment and factors influencing the investment decision. Among these factors, political conditions have demonstrated to be one of the leading factors in assessing a company's foreign direct investment in a foreign company.

Interviews and surveys of executives of multinational corporations have found political events to be one of the most important factors in foreign investment decision. In particular, executives cite the stability of the host government and the attitude of the host government toward to foreign investment as most important considerations in the investment decision.

Kobrin claimed the presence of a negative relationship between political instability and foreign direct investment. After controlling for the effect of economic variables on the flow of foreign investment, the statistical result supported the association between political stability and foreign direct investment is more likely to be conspicuous when there is an economically rooted conflict and the government has sufficient administrative capability to indirectly respond to it.

There are a number of political events and constraints which will eventually cause a loss or harm to a business operating in a foreign environment. Nationalisation and expropriation became the greatest fears for foreign companies in the developing world during this era. The impact of politics on business operations has almost always been seen in the negative. Unexpected political activity by guerrilla or other political groups is another means of political risk. Discriminatory taxation, absence of patent protections, and limits on foreign national employment have also crucial impact on international business in foreign country.

This importance of political risk of host country is more significant in tourism investment. Richter states that political instability is of the foremost importance to any investment, but it is of special consequence to tourism because of what is being sold: serenity, leisure, fun and comfort and these can only be marketed under stable conditions. Moreover, hotels, a major form of tourism investment, are unusually vulnerable to political risk due to substantial investments in fixed assets.

For instance, despite recent economic problems in Brazil, hotel development is strong - aimed largely at capturing the huge domestic business traveller segment. As there is effectively no debt financing available as interest rates are too high, most hotel companies are injecting equity funds into projects, sourcing the finance from private equity, pension funds, or development funds.

### *Political Risk*

A rational, sophisticated approach to foreign investment decision process requires a careful examination by the firm of numerous factors which relate to both the general environment of a proposed investment and the specific operating functions of the firm in that environment. A vital element of the environmental analysis is the question of political risk. The majority of studies of dealing with political risk focus on determining the variables composing that specific risk, or aim to find an association between political events and foreign investment. While the significance of political risk is generally acknowledged, the studies aiming to analyse it are too often vague and difficult to examine and apply in practice.

Analysts providing political risk assessments to MNEs have attempted to overcome the problems of accurately predicting future scenarios which incorporate the dualistic, and often incompatible, components of academic theory and business clarity. Numerous political risk analysis approaches are utilised, either by in-house or outside specialists. These range from qualitative, subjective, and discursive briefings by respected "experts" at one end of the spectrum, to quantitative computer-based assessments drawn from a numerical ranking of various societal variables.

The more sophisticated quantitative approaches are not significantly different from econometric forecasting used by economists; however, political risk analysis instead tracks political trends with multivariate data analysis techniques. Rummel and Heenan integrate objective and subjective methodologies which allows for the best features of management science to be combined with insights and intuition of regional experts.

In political risk studies, generic approach can cause inaccurate determinants. As Erol stated traditional studies assessing political risk and its relation with foreign investment have contemporarily taken into consideration a variety of data from different countries and industries. This generic perspective has led to a failure in determining reliable assessments of the dimension of political risk and its relationship with investments from outside the host country.

The author maintains that political risk assessment must address both the peculiar characteristics of the host country and attribute of the investment project. The project play plays a critical role in determining potential risks because different projects can be differently affected by the political events of a host country. Interestingly some industry types may be more vulnerable than others to specific problems in a country's political economy, especially if political stability is the major concern.

The study led by Fathei - Sedeh and Safizadeli has found that multinational corporations belonging to different industries do not perceive the same degree of risk when facing the same political turmoil in a given country. Hence, in order to identify and assess political risk in international hotel investment, a new framework based on the specific variables of the hotel business and its unique characteristics is necessary.

### *Assessment of Political Risk*

While the threat of political risk warrants such concern, it is not a mystical phenomenon and it susceptible to objective analysis. Indeed, such analysis is already being conducted by a relatively small number of firms. However, the accurate evaluation and comparison of political climates is largely an immature art for businessmen.

The assessment of political risk and more importantly, investment decisions, depend upon prevailing attitudes, first impressions, and generalisation on single events occurring in the host country. Also, according to Kobrin most managers' understanding of the concept of political risk, their assessment and evaluation of politics, and the manner in which they integrate political information into decision making are all rather general, unsophisticated, subjective, and superficial.

Many empirical studies supported that the evaluation of political risk is based on generalisation and impressionistic knowledge of a developing nations. The finding of Keegan indicates the executive responsible for international operations of multinational companies rely very little on systematic environmental scanning methods. Similar findings were reported by Root. The findings indicated that executives' attitudes play a major role in their evaluation of risk and profitability of the investment opportunities.

Most previous empirical studies assumed that the relevant factors for the measurement of political risk could be adequately captured with archival data. In doing so, researchers disregard the crucial role of the perception of decision makers. Irrespective of the actual circumstances, as Rummel and Heenan suggest the forecasts of the underlying factors on which the predictions are based are frequently judgmental so decision makers take decisions that are based on their own judgement of the situation. Ignoring the decisive influence of perception is a weakness in most political risk studies. Hence, the present study recognises the relevance of perception and risk assessment and a survey will be conducted to obtain data from decision makers and experts.

Despite the value of political risk analysis, a few frameworks have been proposed to measure country's political risk. However, there is no consistent framework in the way that the international hotel companies can use to evaluate political risk of foreign country when they intend to make foreign investment decision. Though there are numerous variables are existing in determining a country's political risk, not all of them are taking into consideration of decision -makers.

While some variables may be considered more important for some decision-maker, the others are ignored when they determine a country's political risk. Moreover, each determinant may have different degrees of influence on decision making due to the perception. Hence, it will be interesting to identify the important political indicators in hotel development decision making.

# 8

# Modern Pricing Models

Historically, pricing was pretty straightforward. Pricing was set at one rate, Rack Rate. Those rates were posted on cards and placed in racks at the front desk. As technology became more sophisticated and hoteliers became more marketing savvy, market segments began to evolve. Each segment had its own buy decision and its own travel trends. An in-depth understanding and skillful integration of those segments placed the hotel in a greater position to maximise rates and occupancies. This was all made more manageable by the improved high tech nature of the newer hotel operating systems.

As the new technology was developing, corporate travel departments, as well as the independent consumer, turned to travel agents to get the best discounts. As the GDS technology influenced booking and buying practices, additional segments were created, resulting in the following market segment model:

— *Rack Rates*: Without any affiliations to warrant discounts, the Rack Rated customer paid the published rate, which was the highest rate.

— *Consortia Rates*: This was the same customer who booked through a travel agent using the GDS and received a 5%-10% discount off Rack Rates.

— *Corporate Rates*: Having met the hotel's qualifying criteria, such as volume, businesses were guaranteed discounted rates.

— *Group Rates*: With a block of rooms, rates varied based on time of year and the nature of the group.

— *Weekend Rates*: Individual leisure travellers, usually within a drive distance to the hotel.

— *Promotional rates*: These rates were originally used sparingly and used as a means to stimulate business by using discounted rates to anyone, regardless of affiliation.

By understanding each segment and its role in the individual hotel, hoteliers created pricing and yield management systems and procedures which resulted in maximum performance.

— Rack rates were set to establish positioning; used as a basis for discounting; and used as a yield management tool for average rate maximisation during high demand.

— Consortia rates were typically discounted 5%-10% off Rack Rates in order to capture a savvy traveller educated to ask for discounts through his/her travel agent, and to strengthen the travel agent's value to the customer.

— Corporate rates were negotiated to get year-round volume business for corporate accounts.

— Group rates were usually filler business and negotiated based on demand periods.

— Promotional rates were typically the lowest rates offered and are now being used on a daily basis.

But, as demand dramatically declined, independent hotels were most significantly impacted. In most cases, they did not have the financial resources and cooperative marketing opportunities of the chains. At the same time, the third party Internet booking companies were well positioned. Customer buying habits had changed significantly. As customers began to feel more secure in buying products and services online, use of the Internet become a tremendous resource for the consumer. As the third party Internet companies grew in popularity, independent hotels found a new source of business, with little expense involved.

The Internet has created brand new distribution channels, directly reaching the end user and/or allowing the third party booking parties to profit as travel agents did until recently. The Internet booking companies, in order to ensure profitability, have adopted more of the airline pricing strategy, i.e. setting rates on a daily basis. These rates can vary significantly from day to day. The hotel industry will be hard pressed to revert to the old pricing model, now that the public has been conditioned to shop for prices.

Therefore, in order to respond to the changed market place relative to the Internet and to effectively compete against chain hotels as well as other independent hotels, flexible pricing is key. But in order for hotels to create and maintain pricing credibility, it is still important for hotels to move away from competing on price alone. This strategy has been universally unsuccessful and will always backfire.

Some suggested steps to realign rates and segments to the changed market place; gain control of business; and increase profitability are:

— Create an online booking presence.
— Ensure that the hotel's online booking engine is part of the hotel's web site, and controlled by the hotel, not by a third party or GDS-based system.
— Ensure that the online booking engine is the best and accomplishes the hotel's goals.

— Ensure that the online booking engine is easy to use from a customer's perspective.

— Expertly create and maintain an online distribution and maximisation strategy to ensure the hotel's visibility.

— Promote and ensure that the lowest published rates are on the hotel's own web site, to promote customer loyalty, as done with the airlines.

— Establish a new market segmentation model, for greater control of the business. Eliminate RACK RATE and replace with SELL RATE, defined as Rack, Promotional, Consortia, and any other customer not affiliated with any discount.

— A simplified sample version is:

  — Sell Rate

  — Corporate Rate

  — Group Rate

  — Weekend Rate

— Establish the Sell Rate based on anticipated demand patterns, after the core business and group blocks are factored in. The rate fluctuates on a daily basis.

— Set rates in all market segments within the range of your competitive set to establish positioning.

By understanding how the Internet and customer buying habits have forever changed and how they impact the way hotels do business, will place owners and managers in a position of strength in managing the day to day business; achieving profitability; and demystifying many of the rate and segmentation questions.

### Revenue Management and Pricing

Many readers who were around during the dismal late 80's know only too well what lengths hotel companies will go to in order to save a buck. Nothing wrong with that, right, in the name of business, it's all about money, profit, bottom Line. And their were two ugly words in particular, that seemed to capture the essence of the drastic measures hotels would take to increase sales: RATE WAR. Because of those hard times and the mostly negative impact rate games had on hotel revenues, today's yield strategies are carefully employing tactics to ensure that everything is done to protect revenues and build sales..everything, that is, except price under-cutting.

When profits are down, a hotel can do one of two things to increase RevPAR over last year: Cut Expenses or Increase Sales. Expenses can be cut rather simplistically-make a list of all unnecessary expenses and put the freeze on spending. Unfortunately the subject of sales will be more the challenge for most, as revenues have peaked in the last few years, making achieving those same levels of growth difficult to keep up with.

Dissecting the two components that make up RevPAR, Rate and Occupancy, both at the surface seem unshakable in terms of increasing- after all, demand has "plateaued" in most markets already, and the rate growth which was a phenomenon for so long ('97-2000), has since slowed considerably. With rate protected from significant decrease, hotels may be able to salvage any unnecessary dramatic decrease in RevPAR.

If revenues are going to be down, than let's make sure your revenues are down just as much as your competitors. Keeping up with the Pace of growth of your competitor was important when RevPAR growth was in the double-digits, so why shouldn't it be just as important when RevPAR growth is tepid? You were right to want to grow rate and RevPAR as aggressively as everyone else when times were good, so should you be now, when times are less than desirable: All negative growth is not the same! Let's say your competitor shows a – 2.8% RevPAR decrease over the same month last year. It would be wrong to assume you're doing "just as bad" if you show a – 8% decrease. The latter suggests some money left on the table, for your sales pace worsened significantly more than your competitor.

Pay special attention to the pace of rate growth. On the STAR or HRM (HotelRevMax) Report, note the comparison in percent change period-over-period of your hotel's Average rate vs. your competitive set. While RevPAR might be down, it's important to acknowledge how your competitors are adjusting prices in response to a slowing economy. You might be surprised to notice more of a decrease in occupancy than in rate growth driving any RevPAR decrease.

If softening up on rates seems to be how your market of hotels is reacting to a slowing economy, be sure you identify the pricing strategy being employed by most. There's a fine line between lowering rates across the board and merely allocating additional inventory or rate types available that otherwise would not have been available during those same time periods. An example would be traditionally lower weekend rates being allocated through the midweek, or perhaps a discounted rate attached to a several-night stay. The Yield Management systems used by large hotel companies today make these combination possibilities materialise into camouflaged length-of-stay packages which on the surface might seem impossible to detect of your competitors without some deeper investigating.

When RevPAR growth is in jeopardy, one of the first inclinations of a hotelier might well be to slow, or even stop spending altogether. This is the first mistake. While it is normally prudent to maintain a frugal disposition during slow times, be careful that any revenue management tool which allows you to maintain an "ultra-competitive" position in your market is coveted for the protection it allows: Specifically, in monitoring competitor pricing and inventory controls so that you can implement yield strategies accordingly.

Industry reports, such as STAR and HotelRevMax offer general strategy direction and are indispensable during all demand periods. Industry pricing and GDS reports allow for real-time rate maneauvering and fluctuating. Examples of these valuable pricing and GDS reports would include the long-standing PHASER, Hotelligence, and newcomer Internet pricing report, CHECK-RATE. Increased participation on Price-Line and Expedia are also suggested, with careful thought going into the rate, time period, and product offerings made available.

## Internet Intelligence Report

### *Traditional Distribution Reports*

Traditional vendors continue to provide the current landscape of intelligence distribution reports and focus primarily on the GDS. Recently some of these vendors added online distribution sections supplementary to their predominantly GDS reports. Unfortunately these reports offer hoteliers only a fraction of the big picture of online distribution—Pricing.

These rate-focused reports, like all GDS oriented reports, deal primarily with the daily rate information across online services— helpful but only a fraction of the information hoteliers realistically need to compete online. Especially since most online hotel bookings don't even come from the GDS but through merchant programs or Internet only reservation systems.

These reports provide little analysis on how hoteliers can increase market share, re-gain control of their online pricing from online discounters, or how to utilise direct-to-consumer channels as opposed to merchant services. Sadly, these reports implicitly suggest overuse of intermediaries at the expense of the hotel's own direct distribution strategy. If anything, these reports have aided and abetted those intermediaries to become the 800-pound gorillas of today.

When it comes to the Internet, here are the two most critical questions that should be addressed and that are curiously absent from the traditional distribution intelligence reports:

— Price vs. Positioning on the Web

— Direct vs. Indirect online channel utilisation

Intelligence information for online distribution must delineate direct from indirect channels. A direct channel results in customers booking directly from the hotel's own website while indirect channels, naturally, are the intermediaries. Intelligence information must also include hotel positioning on major direct and indirect channels. Where the hotel ranks on an online service may make or break your entire online distribution strategy. Lastly, such valuable information requires professional analysis with commentary on steps to act or NOT act based on the competitive information being presented.

A sensible Internet intelligence report will offer:

— Tools to help re-gain control of online pricing from online discounters

— Strategies to leverage direct-to-consumer channels over merchant services

— Formulas to balance direct with indirect distribution for optimal results

— Methods to increase market share online

— Invaluable commentary that will teach hoteliers to implement a direct versus indirect distribution strategy

— Needed comparative information to act or not act based on intelligence delivered and action plan for the future

The Internet is the best direct distribution medium ever created. Online hotel sales grew 49% in 2002 to reach above $6 billion, according to PhoCusWright. By 2005, conservative estimates project that nearly a quarter of all rooms will be booked through the web.

*Price and Positioning*

Traditional intelligence reports provide GDS pricing data but do not address the critical question of positioning of hotels on major online agency/intermediary services and the search engines. Hoteliers need positioning information in order to make sound and effective marketing judgments. The order in which the hotel appears on a search engine or online travel agency/intermediary website is of absolute importance otherwise no one will find your hotel rates.

Here's what Bear Stearns analysts say about Internet positioning on major distribution channels: "Our research uncovered that being listed in the top five assures the highest level of bookings, and that after the fifth slot, bookings drop dramatically." Survey after survey confirms the existence of the so called "50% Factor"—roughly 50% of people that visit the first page go to the 2nd page, and only 50% of the people that land on the 2nd page go to the third page, and so on."

The "online purchasing behaviour" is extremely important to keep top of mind when exploiting any competing hotel's Internet strategy. Here are three scenarios to illustrate the importance of positioning over pricing:

— If a competitor's website lists a Web-only special that is $50 lower than yours, do you have to match it? It depends. If your competitor's website is nowhere to be found on the search engines, you should simply ignore it —nobody will see this Web-only special anyway.

— If a hotel appears on Expedia as part of its merchant program and is listed among the top 1-2 pages, the hotel should expect more bookings than its competitor listed on Page 12 as part of Expedia's supplementary hotel inventory feed via Worldspan. Indeed Expedia reports 85% of its hotel revenues generated through its merchant program, which does not utilise the GDS. A traditional distribution report will never capture this critical information.

— If a main competitor aggressively uses Pay-Per-Click marketing and its sponsored links appear on top of the search results, the question then becomes whether to follow suit.

### *Utilisation of Direct and Indirect Online Channel*

Roughly 52% of all online bookings in 2002-2003 will be completed directly through hotel-sponsored websites. If your hotel is not generating at least 52% of its online bookings directly from the hotel website then you are not competitive on the Web and run the risk of long term price and brand erosion caused by the intermediaries. The foundation of a direct distribution strategy begins with an optimised hotel website and includes such important items as enhanced user experience, features that improve conversion rates, customer capture data on and offline, and optimised website navigation and body copy—essential for the search engines.

Direct distribution is so important because the Internet is the ultimate "Direct Distribution Medium". It provides the hotel with long-term competitive advantages and lessens dependence on intermediaries, online discounters, and traditional channels about to become obsolete.

Direct-to-consumer online distribution has the following benefits:

— Puts the hotel in control of its Internet presence and rate exposure

— Prevents brand and price erosion

— Is the shortest path to establishing interactive relationships with customers

— Provides long-term opportunities to benefit from the lifetime customer value

— Is the least expensive way to distribute hotel inventory

Therefore, determining how your website and online direct distribution model compares with your comp set is necessary long term for all those reasons listed above. Don't overlook or underestimate the value of a direct distribution strategy from leveraging many online channels, including major search engines, pay-per-click services, email marketing, and so on.

## Ideal Internet Competitive Report

Such a report would evaluate hotel and its comp set's position and visibility in Cyberspace and measure performance on various online channels. It would measure up the hotel with its competitive set evaluating the use of the direct vs. the indirect online channels—offering pricing and positioning information.

It will determine if the hotel's online distribution is skewed toward indirect channels to the detriment of the hotel brand and price integrity. It would compare website to website, ranking on search engines and utilisation of the direct channel, as well as pricing and positioning on major third-party channels. Frankly, such an ideal report does exist. This report is competitively priced and called the Internet Distribution Monitor (**IDM**) Report.

*IDM Report*

The IDM Report offers easy to read tables, commentary, analysis and concrete recommendations:

— Compares the utilisation of Direct vs. Indirect distribution channels
— Identifies major channels being used and not used by hotel and competitive hotels
— Informs hoteliers on product pricing and positioning on all major distribution channels
— Compares your website to your competitive set on functionality, usability, and best practices, focusing on features that boost the conversion rates (look-to-book ratio), add credibility and make the website search engine friendly.
— Identifies and compares hotel website on all major search engines and PPC services
— Compares rates and positioning in the indirect channel: merchant, opaque and agency services
— Offers timely information formatted in monthly, quarterly and annual reports
— Delivers brand and property level reports
— Tracks any competitive set, size of set, in any market and group of markets anywhere in the world
— Best of all—easy to read, personalized, concise, and highly informative 20-page report offering commentary, analysis and recommendations to act or NOT act based on the intelligence collected

### *Direct Distribution Channel*

The Direct Web Distribution is all about benefiting from the Internet as the greatest direct-to-consumer distribution medium. Direct online distribution should become the centerpiece of any hotel's Internet strategy. The most important direct channel is your website. Determine how your website measures up to your competitors, and compare listings on the major direct channels: search engines and pay-per-click services.

Direct distribution section covers:

— 17-point website functionality comparison
— Search engine ranking (positioning)
— Pay-per-click (PPC) marketing services utilisation and positioning
— Proprietary CyberScore system to evaluate the hotel utilisation of the direct channel
— Analysis and Recommendations

### *Indirect Channels*

Compare pricing and positioning on the most popular indirect distribution channels. Know which indirect channels are used by your hotel and comp set. Make sure visitors to these well-trafficked websites can find you. Set your pricing strategy with the full picture: Pricing and Positioning.

Indirect distribution section covers:

— Merchant channels
— Agency channels
— Opaque channels
— Proprietary CyberScore system to evaluate the hotel utilisation of the indirect channel
— Analysis and Recommendations

# 9

# Hotel Revenue Management

Revenue Management (RM) is more complex than ever and changes in the discipline are morphing at light speed. RM not only manages demand during peak periods but also has a huge impact on stimulating demand in shoulder seasons. RM no longer only applies to room revenue but to managing the potential revenue for all profit centers. It enables a smart Customer Relationship Management strategy that has the potential to stimulate demand from the most valuable guests.

The position of the General Manager is one of juggling competing priorities, keeping the department heads from seriously hurting each other and at the same time trying to produce an exceptional guest experience. What's a GM to do to ramp up the Revenue Management IQ? Below are a few areas to test your RM IQ.

— *Understand the Reports*: Your Revenue Manager probably produces a plethora of reports and proudly gives them to you during the Revenue Management meeting. The reports come from various sources including the PMS, the GDS, the various channels and franchise reports. The Revenue Manager has probably designed a few of their own. Stare at them until they begin to make sense, ask for explanations and don't pretend that you understand them when you don't.

— *Daily, Weekly and Monthly Disciplines*: This is key to understanding what your Revenue Manager does all day. There is a set of activities that need to be performed at these intervals. Know what they are – how else can you measure how well the Revenue Manager is executing the RM strategy.

— *Channel Management*: We now refer to channels as all sources of reservations. If you still think this refers only to the Internet travel sites, you need to ramp up. Managing these channels is more than just turning the inventory and rate faucet on and off, it also includes merchant agreements, internet specials, GDS marketing etc, to stimulate demand. This is a critical area for your Revenue Manager.

— *Web Site*: Especially if you are managing an independent hotel or resort, you as a GM need to understand site design, optimization and Internet marketing. This is critical to the success of any independent. Your Revenue Manager should be intimately involved with the design and functionality of the reservation engine on your site.

— *Rate Strategy versus Pricing Strategy*: The rate strategy is where you position your rate structure for the year or fiscal period. The pricing strategy includes closing discounts, rates for 'hot dates' etc., in the short term or within the period covered by the rate strategy.

— *Revenue Management and Customer Relationship Management*: This tends to produce the glazed over 'deer in the headlights' look. The simple explanation is that CRM is about identifying the value of customers, individually or by market segment and then developing relationships with them in order to secure their loyalty or, put simply, repeat business. It can be this simple or much more complex but GMs need to understand what this means and the implications for the future.

## Feeding the Elephant of Hotel Revenue

Hoteliers who blindly accept the demand that comes their way at the rate they ask will never know how good it could have been had they fed the elephant of hotel revenue with guests that were not measure solely by rate but by value.

Amitava Chatterhjee in the upcoming edition of Hospitality Upgrade has an excellent article that states, "..a 2% increase in customer retention is equivalent to a 10% reduction in costs." He goes on to say that "... hospitality enterprises (should) start measuring and tracking a guests profitability "

How much money are you leaving on the table? How many of the customers that you get this summer at the rate you are asking will never return? How many of them are not the demographic that will feed the revenue elephant in the future? How much does it cost you when you squeeze out the high value customer for the 'one night stand' at a higher rate? What is the cost of constantly appealing to those customers without the potential to return?

So what does this have to do with Revenue Management – everything! Most revenue management proponents, advocate measuring the value of a guest not just in terms of room rate or REVPAR but also in terms of potential for other profit centers such as F&B, the spa, other attractions within the hotel or facility. This is a revenue management function. The more sophisticated revenue management systems can drill this down relatively easily. For those of you who are doing it the 'old fashioned way' it isn't impossible – just a bit more work.

— *Capturing the Information*: This is a training issue with the front desk/reservations. Many GMs say 'I tell them to do that' – there is a huge difference between 'telling' and 'training'. Email addresses offer a fast, cheap and easy way to cement guest relationships. There are several points at which you can capture this information – ask at check in or check out or on a 'permission' box on your web site.

— *Email Guest Comment Surveys*: This is a rationale for asking the guest for their email addresses upon check in or departure. If you are not using this medium now, it is readily available through companies that perform this function or easily accomplished by someone who is relatively familiar with technology. The studies indicate that guests are more likely to respond to email surveys than to a survey mailed to them. The survey also contains a section where permission is given to receive occasional promotions from the guest.

— *Capturing the Identity of Guests Booked by the Distribution Systems*: The guest that arrives and departs that has booked through a travel portal is invisible to the hotel in terms of market segment or demographics unless we capture the information at check in or check out. If we can get them into our system, we can develop relationships with them.

— *The Functionality of the PMS System*: Most PMS systems are capturing guest information that can then be sliced by demographics such as when they stayed, for how many nights, total bill at checkout, etc. The problem is that many hotel GMs and DOSs aren't aware of this or how to access it. This info can be use to target certain guest demographics at times of the year when they are most likely to be making reservations. It can be used for all market segments and the promotions can be used for email postcards and flyers or mailings in the absence of email addresses.

Many of you are now thinking that this involves CRM, Customer Relationship Mangement. This is a term that either provokes the 'glazed over eyes' or total 'brain lock' for many hoteliers. Determining the 'value of a guest', many find it difficult to get their minds around it. Most of you are now thinking, "It's summer, I'm too busy to worry about this stuff ". Capturing the information now will enable you to use it later.

Most franchises focus their efforts on their frequent guests for whom they are able to collect this information relatively easily. However, there is a segment of guest, such as leisure, that may not be a member of the frequent guest programme but whose business is valuable and can be targeted from the property level. If you are waiting for the franchise to do all this work for you, you are missing the boat.

This is especially critical for independent hotels. The CRM process is not difficult but needs to be thought out and become a part of the overall marketing and revenue management strategy. It is the most 'valuable' guests that feed the Revenue Management elephant most profitably. The cost of CRM in feeding the elephant is far lower than the cost associated with most of the other reservation channels.

As peak season nears for many hotels, revenue management is the key to a successful summer season. Leisure remains strong even as business travel continues to disappoint and it is imperative that in March the pieces are in place to maximize revenue. Potential customers are much smarter than they used to be about locating, qualifying and making their hotel choice. In many cases, this process is completed without ever contacting the hotel.

The term revenue management means many things to different people — whatever the definition, the intended end result of the process is increased REVPAR for the organization. Revenue drivers are defined as all areas of revenue generation within the organization. This includes central reservations, property-level reservations, the sales department, the electronic distribution channels and the web site. While franchised properties have a higher level of consistency through the GDS, it still requires monitoring and management at the company or property levels.

At a recent sales seminar, participants expressed frustration that they are largely unaware of, nor are they consulted about the rates that are posted on the electronic distribution channels. One result is a very high attrition rate in meetings and conventions as attendees book their hotel at these lower rates and "fall" off the group block. Another consequence is when the rate posted is lower than what has been negotiated with third-party suppliers such as wholesalers. A coaching client of mine expressed frustration over his lack of consultation in the development of the new property web site and the rates that are being quoted through the site.

First of all, the content was skewed to a specific market segment that was not representative of the core business segment and secondly, the copy changes disrupted the optimization strategy. Secondly, the rates that were quoted were not at all aligned with the rates being quoted at the property level or through the central reservations agent and many room descriptions were inaccurate. The end result was that not only was this hotel no where to be found on the key word searches in the major search engines — a potential disaster for this independent property, but fewer reservations were being made through the site.

Collaboration across all departments that generate revenue is the only way to ensure continuity. This need not be a tedious process of endless meetings. A few things put into place and adjusted periodically, based on market conditions and forecasts, are sufficient:

— *Product/Rate Positioning*: A plan for product/rate positioning is ideally developed as part of the Business/Marketing plan process and includes consideration of the product/rate positioning of the competitive set, group bookings, rate resistance input from reservations and past history. Once the strategy is developed, it then only needs to be adjusted periodically. Don't forget to monitor the franchise yield management system in light of groups or events in previous years that may not be a factor in the present year.

— *Existing and Anticipated Contracts*: These include group contracts, volume contracts with LNRs, wholesalers and any other rate commitments. Just as the sales department makes decisions based on the rate structure, so should consideration be given to any agreements made thorough sales. It is one thing to adjust rates on the web site or distribution channels to drive volume at a slow time but if it undermines the agreements above, it is counter productive.

— *Web Site Presence and Reservations*: Many leisure customers locate the hotel through key word searches on the search engines. Others locate the hotel on the electronic distribution channels then access the hotel's proprietary web site. Still others will pick up the phone after visiting both and call reservations to see if they can cut a better deal. It is essential that the "message" of rate and offering be relatively consistent across all channels to be effective. The rates on the web site need to be adjusted in tandem with the electronic distribution channels and reservations needs to be aware of what's appearing on both.

Another consideration in web site development is the increased use of the site as a sales tool. It becomes the electronic brochure. The sales department's inclusion in its development is essential to the site's secondary role as the electronic brochure. Sales people should be accessing the site with their clients to moderate the virtual tour. If there is a special rate posted that is inconsistent with the rates sales are quoting, it blows them out of the water and appears to the client that the hotel doesn't know what it is doing.

The process of collecting the information is about communication and collaboration and can be accomplished through periodic updates from the revenue drivers to the revenue management team. This swings both ways as revenue management needs to keep the revenue drivers informed of their proposed tactics in order to solicit input and buy in.

The consequence of not doing this is to present an inconsistent message to the public who is in the position of making selections without any direct contact with the property thus depriving the hotel from any opportunity to make adjustments or explain the disconnect. In the consumer's mind, a hotel that can't get its act together to project consistent rates may have the same problem when it comes to servicing them as guests. The issue is more than rate parity, it is aligning the rate structures between all revenue generating departments so that each is maximizing their contribution to revenue.

## Robust Revenue Management Systems

Robust Revenue Management systems have been the drivers behind the industry's ability to drive ADR and

REVPAR in 2004 and will continue to be the drivers for the foreseeable future. Consider the following forecast from PKF. Demand is expected to increase by 2.8%. Supply is anticipated to increase by only 1.6% but ADR is forecasted to increase by a whopping 4.7% resulting in an average REVPAR increase of between 7.7 and 8.4% in 2005.

"In 2005, ADR will be the main driver of REVPAR improvements," says (R. Mark) Woodworth. (Mr. Woodworth is the Executive Managing Director of the Hospitality Research Group of PKF Consulting, author of Perspectives on the Road to Recovery, US Lodging Industry 2005, HRG/PKF, HotelOnline, November 2004.)

In a typical urban/suburban mid level corporate transient property, the mid-week peaks are dominated by business travellers whose rate sensitivity is less as they, individually, are not paying the bill. While corporate travel departments are continuing to try and manage the cost of travel, the reality is that in prime locations, room rates are increasing and they find themselves negotiating higher rates in their RFPs than in previous years.

Another factor to consider is that bookings from all electronic sources have increased another 30-40% from 2003. This includes all channels from the GDS systems, e-commerce channels and the franchise web site. These bookings are also driven by an increase in leisure travel that has been induced by the lowest airfares in a decade. While airfares remain low, this segment demonstrated in the summer of 2004 that they were willing to pay higher hotel rates than in past years.

The dilemma for hotel sales departments is to locate and manage group business to fill in the blanks mid-week and weekends, often from market segments and demand generators that press for lower rates. They also are dealing with third party meeting planners attempting to negotiate the best (read lowest) rates for their clients. The Revenue Manager is pressing for a higher rate, group booking contacts are pressing for lower rates and the sales person is under pressure to meet their booking goals — it is a stressful situation for the sales department!

The solutions are varied but hinge upon the ability of the sales person and department to understand and be able to measure the impact of potential bookings and rates upon the hotel's revenue management strategy. Once they understand those parameters, they can then align their new business development activities in relation to the client profiles that fit the revenue management model.

It is both the lack of understanding and/or the inability to measure their potential contracts prior to negotiating and booking that provokes the criticism that "sales only wants to book the lowest rates." They will stand their ground if given the tools in order to, first of all, develop new business in line with the revenue management strategy and secondly, measure the value of a group to the hotel's top line. In other words, understand the difference between good business and bad. The following are a few suggestions:

— *The Revenue Management Strategy*: Those who are involved in developing the strategy have "buy in" to its successful execution. Sales is fine with the understanding that their ADRs for groups during the weekends will remain the same as the past year and maybe even be a bit reduced in order to attract SMERFE business. It is a deal that is cut so that everyone knows what the expectations are. The Revenue Manager is part of the sales team rather than a direct report to the Rooms Division.

— *Develop Client Profiles for Each Rate Period*: In order to be more effective in locating prospects that will fit into the management, it is imperative to know what you are looking for. In other words, which types of groups in market segments and sub segments will fit within the rate and catering parameters that will align with the revenue management strategy. Attempting to meet these goals through only responding to telephone inquiries and working the trace files is insufficient to attain the goals. First of all, there is no control over the kind of prospects calling and the pressure builds to respond to their requests if this is your only means of prospecting. Secondly, the accounts in the trace files may or may not be in alignment with the new revenue goals in terms of rates and meeting configurations. A client profile should be driven by market segment, where the bookings are likely to originate, their rate sensitivity or history and their meeting configurations. For example, in the SMERFE market, a group of wine enthusiasts may be less rate sensitive and more inclined to spend money on F&B than a group of students. A group originating in a city with a higher ADR may be less rate sensitive than those that originate locally.

— *Develop a New Business Development Strategy*: Once the client profiles are developed, it becomes a matter of developing a strategy to locate and qualify these prospects. Strategies might include using the Internet to locate certain organizations within a market segment from a specific geographic location or getting on an email distribution list or mailing list for organizations that have the potential to produce groups for the hotel is another one. There are web sites that specialize in producing leads for groups for hotels in various market segments. These can be sorted by geographic location and often give the rates, meeting specs and history of where the group last met.

— *Provide a Group Revenue Management Tool*: A revenue management tool can be as simple as a spreadsheet of the group rooms budget by month into which the parameters of the group can be entered so that the sales person can see how the number of rooms at the proposed rate effects the room revenue of the entire hotel for the period. It can be as sophisticated as a computer programme that measures the revenue of a group on all profit centers. These take various forms and often are included with the sales contact management system such as the ones offered by Delphi. Some of these products interface with the property's PMS and Revenue management systems.

The future of the hotel sales is in being able to first of all, locate groups that fit the revenue management strategy and secondly, measure the viability of a group in the date ranges and rate requested in relation to the hotel's revenue management strategy.

All the signs are there — the economy, for the hotel industry in particular and the country as a whole, is improving. TIA is forecasting an increase of 3.5% in business travel and a 3.2% increase in domestic leisure travel for 2004. This follows an estimated decrease in business travel of 3.7% in 2003 and an increase of 2.8% in domestic leisure travel for this year.

The hotel industry is collectively waiting to exhale. It would appear that business travel is firing up although TIA president and CEO, William S. Norman cautions that "it will be some time before business travel returns to its peak levels of the late 1990s." There is speculation that 2005 will see the industry hitting numbers close to those of 2000, largely considered to be the last good year in the industry.

These are all positive signs. What could possibly go wrong? The conundrum of an improving economy is that new hotel development will increase proportionately. Patrick Ford of Lodging Econometrics, foresees this in an article entitled "Improving Economic conditions Point to a Mid-Decade Development Upswing." The industry has reason for optimism, but will demand improve sufficiently by 2005 to absorb that new supply and will the revenues and profits of 2000 really materialize with increased inventory supplies?

This is of special concern to operators of aging hotel products who may not have been in a position to inject capital into their properties. It is also of concern to those who have because a renovated 20-year-old hotel still has an uphill battle against new hotel product. The bottom line is, can we go back to the days when demand was sufficiently strong and all that was needed was to manage rate and inventory? Will hoteliers be tempted to cling to their rate structures of the boom years and will developers have the "build it and they will come" attitude that was so prevalent during the mid 1990s?

For every new hotel that opens, a re-positioning in the market occurs. The existing hotels have to re-think their positioning strategy in terms of the price/value equation in the mind of the consumer. This requires an honest and agonizing re-appraisal of the property in relation to the new products entering the market. Stubbornly maintaining one's rate and incremental increases in the budget is to bury one's head in the sand.

To re-position an existing hotel in the face of new competition requires a comprehensive strategy in terms of value, rate and allocation of sales resources to reflect the shift in the market that will occur. This strategy should also include an evaluation of the franchise affiliation and its alignment with the changes in the market. The process of re-thinking a strategy should include everyone from the ownership, management and sales department. The process should ultimately include the following:

— *Franchise Affiliation*: The proliferation of franchise brands and the reduction of proximity to existing franchisees are issues that the industry as a whole will have to come to terms with. The problem was that there was no franchise available in that market that would be aligned with the new product. Many operators have been in the position of adopting a franchise that they were less than pleased with simply because it was the only one available. How well is the franchise working for the property, does it reflect the product and how well does it assist you in a new competitive situation?

— *Price/Value Equation*: What will be the competitive advantages that a new hotel can exploit to increase its market share? How can an existing hotel build value into its product and rate structure to offset the new competitors strategy? Which benefits of the new property will be appealing to an existing property's guests and how can the existing property offset them?

— *Sales and Marketing Strategies*: This is no time to recycle the marketing plan of years past. Which market segments is the new competitor going to target? Can you identify additional or previously ignored market segments to offset potential inroads into a market segment targeted by the competition? Can you pursue these market segments more effectively by reallocating sales resources, both people and marketing dollars? Can you effectively track the ROI on marketing and sales initiatives that are now in place and any new ones that you envision?

The process is an essential one to conduct. If you don't aggressively take control of the situation then you will be in a position of waiting for demand to increase sufficiently to absorb the new supply so that you can regain market share. That is, if you and your existing hotel can survive long enough for that to happen.

# 10

# Managing Working Capital

Cash is the most liquid asset of all and is vital for existence of any business firm. Its efficient management is crucial to the solvency of the business because as we all know cash is the focal point of the funds flows in a business. It can be understood in two senses, one is actual cash held by firm and deposits withdraw able on demand, and in another sense it includes marketable securities, which can be convertible into cash immediately.

The goal of cash management is to reduce the amount of cash that is being used within the firm so as to increase profitability, but without reducing business activities or exposing the firm to undue risk in its financial obligations. Cash flows in connection with credit serve to introduce the concept of Float which is the time lag or delay between the moment of disbursement of funds on the part of the customer and the moment of receipt of funds on the part of the seller.

Cash in checking accounts must be held so that bills are paid on time (transactions balance), for emergencies such as strikes, weather disruptions, etc. (Precautionary balance), bank requirements for loans or other services provided (Compensating balance), and for taking advantage of bargains (speculative balance).

## Motives for Holding Cash

— *The transaction motive:* Firms are in existence to create products or provide services. The providing of services and creating of products results in the need for cash inflows and outflows. Firms hold cash in order to satisfy the cash inflow and cash outflow needs that they have.

— *The precautionary motive:* Holding cash as a precaution serves as an emergency fund for a firm. If expected cash inflows are not received as expected cash held on a precautionary basis could be used to satisfy short-term obligations that the cash inflow may have been bench marked for.

— *Compensating motive:* Banks provide a variety of services to business firms, such as clearance of cheque, supply of credit..etc., for which a minimum balance is required to be kept with the bank, this balance is to compensate banks for services rendered.

— *The speculative motive:* Economist Keynes described this reason for holding cash as creating the ability for a firm to take advantage of special opportunities that if acted upon quickly will favour the firm.

*Cash management managing of:*

— Cash flows into & out of the firm,

— Cash flows within the firm

— Cash balances held by the firm at a point of time by financing deficit or investing surplus cash.

*Facets of Cash Management*

— Cash planning

— Managing the cash flows

— Optimum cash level
— Investing surplus cash

All of these strategies are explained in the following paragraphs

*Cash planning*

Cash planning is a technique to plan and control the use of cash. It protects the financial condition of the firm by developing a projected cash statement from a forecast of expected cash flows for a given period. It may be done on daily, weekly, or monthly basis.

*Cash forecasting & budgeting:* Cash budget is the most significant device to plan for & control cash receipts & payments. A cash budget is a summary statement of the firm's expected cash inflows & outflows over a projected time period. Cash forecasts are needed to prepare cash budgets. Cash forecasting may be done on short or long term basis.

— Short-term forecasting methods
  — The receipts & disbursement method: The cash flows can be compared with the budgeted income & expense items in this method. The sources of cash flows can be identified:
    — Operating: cash sales & collections from customers
    — Non-operating: sale of old assets & dividend & interest income
    — Financial: when internally generated cash flows are not sufficient, the firm resorts to external sources such as borrowing & issuance of securities.
  — The adjusted net income method: Involves the tracing of working capital flows. Also called as

sources & uses approach. Objectives of this approach can be:

- To project the company's need for cash at a future date
- To show whether the company can generate the required funds internally & if, not, how much it will have to borrow or raise funds in the capital market.

— Long-term cash forecasting:

- To give an idea of the company's cash requirements in the distant future
- Uses:
  - Indicate company's future cash needs.
  - Helps to evaluate proposed capital projects
  - Helps to improve corporate planning.

*Ways to Manage Cash*

Firms can manage cash in virtually all areas of operations that involve the use of cash. The goal is to receive cash as soon as possible while at the same time waiting to pay out cash as long as possible. The two objectives in managing cash flows are:

— *Accelerating cash collections:* The amounts of cheque sent by customer, which are not yet collected, are called collection or deposit float. Within this time the delay is caused by the mailing time i.e. the time taken by the cheque in transit and the processing time i.e. the time taken by the firm in processing the cheque for internal accounting purposes. This also depends on the processing time taken by the banks well as the inter bank system to get credit in the desired account. The greater the firms deposit float, the longer the time taken in converting cheque into usable funds. Attempt should be made to reduce the firm' deposit float by speeding up the mailing, processing & collection times.

— How to accelerate cash collections?

— Decentralised collections

— Lock-box system

— Prompt payment by Customers

— Early conversion of payment into cash

## Cash Management Objectives

The financial manager must know as to why the cash management is a necessity. The cash management strategies are generally built around two goals:

— To provide cash needed to meet the obligations, and

— To minimize the idle cash held by the firm.

The financial manager has to strike an acceptable balance between holding too much cash and too little cash. This is the focal point of the cash risk-return trade-off. A large cash investment minimizes the chances of default but penalizes the profitability of the firm. A small cash balance target may free the excess cash balance for investment in marketable securities and thereby enhancing the profitability as well as value of the firm, but increases simultaneously the chances of running out of cash. The risk-return trade-off of any firm can be reduced to two prime objectives for the firm's cash management system, as follows:

### *Meeting the Cash Outflows*

The primary objective of cash management is to ensure the cash outflows, as and when required. Enough cash must be on hand to meet the disbursal needs that arise in the normal course of business. The firm should be able to make the payments at different point of time without any liquidity problem. It means that the firm should have sufficient cash to meet the payment schedules and disbursement needs. It will help the firm in

— avoiding the chance of default in meeting financial obligations, otherwise the goodwill of the firm is adversely affected,
— availing the opportunities of getting cash discounts by making early or prompt payments, and
— meeting unexpected cash outflows without much problem.

### *Minimizing the Cash Balance*

Investment in idle cash balance must be reduced to a minimum. This objective of cash management is based on the idea that unused asset earns no income for the firm. The funds locked up in cash balance are a dead investment and has no earning. Therefore, whatever cash balance is maintained, the firm is foregoing interest income on that balance.

The objective of the cash management therefore, should be to keep minimum cash balance. However, the objective of cash management i.e., maintaining the minimum cash balance must be looked into together with the other objectives i.e., maintaining the payment schedule etc., which require that a firm must have sufficient liquidity (even at the cost of-reducing profitability). But the objective of minimum cash balance affects the liquidity and thereby increasing the profitability. Thus, these objectives seem to be contradictory in nature and hence the financial manager has to achieve a trade-off between them. He has to ensure that the minimum cash balance being maintained by the firm is not affecting the payment schedule and meeting all disbursement needs. The cash management strategies are needed to reconcile these two goals wherever possible. However, meeting payment commitments takes higher priority than minimizing the cash balance.

## Improve Collection of Cash

### *Changing Customer Paying Habits*

— Letters, telephone calls, or personal visits

— Economic incentive for paying bills faster; offer discounts

### *Improve the Delivery System*

— Regional banking (customers pay bills to banks since they can transfer funds more quickly than mail order delivery).

— Lockbox collection system (firm rents a post office box in a particular city and the bank monitors the lockbox periodically).

— Electronic communications (i.e., data-phone wire systems).

### *Bypass the Problem*

— There is no advantage in paying sooner than agreed. By delaying payments much as possible, the firm makes maximum use of trade credit as a source of funds- a source which is interest free

— Disbursement or payment float: is defined as the difference between the book balance and the bank balance of an account. For example, assume that you go to the bank and open a checking account with $500. You receive no interest on the $500 and pay no fee to have the account. Now assume that you receive your water bill in the mail and that it is for $100. You write a check for $100 and mail it to the water company. At the time you write the $100 check you also record the payment in your bank register. Your bank register reflects the book value of the checking account. The check will literally be "in the mail" for a few days before it is received by the water company and may go several more days before the water company cashes it. The time between the moment you write the check and the time the bank cashes the check there is a difference in your book balance and the balance the bank lists for your checking account. That difference is float. This float can be managed. If you know that the bank will not learn about your check for five days, you could take the $100 and invest it in a savings account at the bank for the five days and then place it back into your checking account "just in time" to cover the $100 check.

### *Determining the Optimum Cash Balance*

#### *Baumol's model*

This model considers cash management similar to an inventory management's problem.

- Assumptions of Baumol's model
    - The firm is able to forecast it cash need with certainty
    - The firms cash payments occur uniformly over a period of time
    - The opportunity cost of holding cash is known and it does not change over a period of time
    - The firm will incur the same transaction cost whenever it converts its securities to cash.

— Limitations of Baumol's model: It does not allow the ash flows to fluctuate. Firms in practice do not use their cash balance uniformly nor they are able to predict daily cash inflows and outflows.

*Optimum Cash Balance under uncertainty*

*Miller-Orr Model:* The Miller-Orr Model overcomes the shortcomings present in the Baumol's model. It assumes that net cash flows are normally distributed with a zero value of mean & standard deviation. The MO model provides for two control limits -the upper control limit & the lower control limit as well as the return point. If the firm's cash flow fluctuate randomly and hit the upper limit, then it buys sufficient marketable securities to come back to a normal level of cash balance (return point). Similarly, when the firm's cash flows wander and hit the lower limit, it sells sufficient marketable securities to bring the cash balance back to the normal level (return point).

***Short-Term Investment Opportunities***

— *Treasury bills*: are short-term government securities. Usually, they are sold at a discount and redeemed at par. The difference is the return on security. They can be bought & sold any time; thus they have liquidity. Also, they do not have the default risk.

— *Commercial papers*: are short-term, unsecured securities issued by highly creditworthy large companies. They are issued with a maturity of three months to one year.

— *Certificates of deposits*: do banks acknowledging fixed deposits for a specific period of time issue papers? They are negotiable instruments that make them marketable securities.

— *Bank deposits*: A firm can deposit its temporary cash in a bank for a fixed period of time. The interest rate depends on the maturity period.

## Management of Working Capital

### *Factors Affecting the Cash Needs*

It has already been said that the financial manager has to achieve a trade-off between liquidity and profitability and in doing so he should note that there are various factor, which will determine the amount of cash balance to be kept by the firm. Some of these factors are as follows:

#### *Cash cycle*

The term cash cycle refers to the length of the time between the payment for purchase of raw material and the receipt of sales revenue. So, the cash cycle refers to the time that elapses from-the point when the firm makes an outlay to purchase raw materials to the point when cash is collected from the sale of finished goods produced using that raw material. Different patterns of cash cycles and cash flows may be there depending upon the nature of the business. The concept of cash cycle has been depicted in the following figure.

#### *Cash inflows and cash outflows*

Every firm has to maintain cash balance because its expected inflows and outflows are not always synchronised. The timings of the cash inflows may not always, match with the timing of the outflows. Therefore, a cash balance is required to fill up the gap arising out of difference in timings and quantum of inflows and outflows. If the inflows are appearing just at the time when cash is required for payment, then no cash balance will be required to be maintained by the firm. But this seldom happens. So, the financial manager has to identify the timings and quantity by which the inflows will not be synchronised with the outflows and an arrangement must be made to fill the gap.

*Cash balance cost*

Another factor to be considered while determining the minimum cash balance is the cost of maintaining excess cash or of meeting shortages of cash. There is always an opportunity cost of maintaining excessive cash balance. If a firm is maintaining excess cash then it is missing the opportunities of investing these funds in a profitable way. Similarly, if the firm is maintaining inadequate cash balance than it may be required to arrange funds on an emergency basis to meet any unexpected shortage. Even if the shortage is expected to continue only for a short period, yet the funds are to be arranged and there will always be a cost (may be more than normal cost) of raising fund.

In addition to the above factors, there may be some other considerations also affecting the need for cash balance. There may be several sub1ective considerations such as uncertainties of a particular trade, staff required for cash management etc., which will have a bearing on determining the cash balance required by a firm.

***Planning Aspect of Cash Management***

In order to maintain an optimum cash balance, what is required is

— A complete and accurate forecast of net cash flows over the planning horizon and

— Perfect synchronisation of cash receipts and disbursements.

Thus, implementation of an efficient cash management system starts with the preparation of a plan of firm's operations for a period in future. This plan will help in preparation of a statement of receipts and disbursements expected at different point of time of that period. It will enable the management to pin point the timing of excessive cash or shortage of cash. This will also help to find out whether there is any expected surplus cash still unutilised or shortage of cash, which is yet to be arranged for; In order to take care of all these considerations, the firm should prepare a cash budget.

A cash budget is a summary of movement of cash during a particular period. There are three methods of preparation of cash budget. These are

— Adjusted Net Income,

— Pro-form a Balance Sheet, and

— Cash Receipts and Disbursements.

In all these methods, the information with which the final cash budget is constructed is basically the same. However, they utilise different forecasting techniques and therefore, the information they provide to the financial manager is quite different.

— *The Adjusted Net Income Method:* Requires that a pro-forma income statement should be prepared for each desired interim period of the budget period. The net income figures for each period are then adjusted to a cash basis by deleting the transactions that are affecting the income statements but not the cash balance or the items, which affect the one without affecting the other. This adjusted figure is taken as cash profit (loss) during that period. This can be taken as net increase or decrease in cash balance during that period.

— *The Pro-forma Balance Sheet Method:* Requires the preparation of as many pro-forma balance sheets as there are interim periods in the cash budget. Each item of the balance sheet except cash is projected for each period, and the cash balance is ascertained in accordance with the accounting equation i.e., Total Assets = Total Liabilities + Capital. The balancing figure of the proforma balance sheet is taken as the cash balance. A negative cash balance or a cash balance falling below minimum desirable balance would, of course, indicate a need for borrowing funds or otherwise adjusting the flow to make up the anticipated shortages of cash.

Both these approaches to the preparation of cash budget tend to limit their use to those firms having stable earnings and sales add also having cash surpluses. First, neither method produces an item-by-item forecast of cash receipts and disbursements, and consequently, it is difficult for the financial manager to plan the timing of the firm's payment closely with its anticipated receipts. Second, the lack of details also makes its difficult to locale an appropriate item for adjusting the timing of cash flows during the budget period. The cash receipts and disbursements is probably the best method of construction of cash budget and has been discussed as follows:

— *Receipts and Payments Method of Cash Budget*: Cash budget, under this method, is a statement projecting the cash inflows and outflows (receipts and disbursements) of the firm over various interim periods of the budget period. For each period, the expected inflows are put against the expected outflows to find out if there is going to be any surplus or deficiency in a particular period. Surplus, if any, during a particular period may be carried forward to the next period or steps may be taken to make short-term investments of this surplus. Deficiencies, if any, must be arranged for within the same period from some short-term sources of finance such as bank credit etc.

The cash budget, under the receipts and payments method may be prepared on a monthly basis or quarterly or half-yearly basis. For every month/quarter/half-year, there is an opening cash balance, expected inflows and expected outflows during that period and a closing balance of cash at the end of that period. The cash inflows may be consisting of all receipts whether from cash sales; or realisation from debtors; or income from investment or sale proceed of any investment or assets; or any loan expected from bank etc.; or a subsidy expected from Government etc.

The cash outflows, on the other hand, may include payment for materials, labour and overheads, taxes dividends and interest, loan repayments, purchase of assets, statutory deposits etc. The cash budget, as the name itself suggests, is prepared on the cash basis (against the accrual basis of accounting) and hence non-cash items such as depreciation expense etc., are ignored.

Under the receipts and payments method of preparation of cash budget, first of all, the cash budget period is selected. A financial year is no doubt the over all period within which smaller interim periods, say a week or a month or a quarter is selected. Now, detailed cash inflows and outflows for each interim period are noted down. Beginning with the opening cash balance, the expected cash inflow during each period is added to it and from the total; the expected outflows for that period are deducted to find out the cash balance at the end of that period. This closing cash balance becomes the opening cash balance of the next period and so on.

All types of expected cash inflows and outflows i.e., transaction cash flows, precautionary cash flows and speculative cash flows are incorporated because all these affect the cash balance required during particular period, and moreover these cash flows are consistently changing from one period to another. The interaction among these three cash flows results in a need to identify the minimum cash balance i.e., desired at any point of time.

While preparing the cash budget, this desired minimum cash balance is considered at the end of each of the cash budget period. If a firm is preparing monthly cash budget, then the cash balance at the end of each month must be equal to the desired cash balance. If not, then arrangements must be made/planned to increase the cash balance at that time by procuring funds from some or the other source.

### *Cash Reports for Monitoring and Control*

The basic advantage of cash budgets, which are nothing but short-term cash forecasts, lies in their amenability for monitoring actual for exercising control. That is the reason why the break—down of the time horizon has been discussed. When cash inflows and outflows do not fluctuate very much and the collection and payment patterns are stabilized, monthly cash reports may serve the purpose. However, when uncertainty surrounding the cash flows, is high, there is need to monitor information on the cash position at more frequent intervals on a weekly or daily basis to keep close watch and to revise the budget for the subsequent period based on the variance between the budgeted and actual figures and the reasons therefore.

In the case of a multi-product multi-branch company it is preferable to have cash budgets as also cash reports both product—wise and branch—wise, apart from the consolidated ones. The daily cash report provides information on the cash position at the beginning and at the end.

While this information is certainly helpful to the finance controller, it does not indicate the position the position of Accounts Receivables, Accounts Payables and that and that of marketable securities, which a company holds. Further, a close watch needs to be maintained on important items that call for mandatory payments such as tax payment, meeting instalments of term loans and their timing. This is necessary as they involve drain on cash resources of considerable magnitude. This shortcoming of the daily, cash report is circumvented by what is known as daily treasury export. This will indicate the opening and closing net treasury positions. The net treasury position is obtained by subtracting Accounts Payable from the sum total of cash, marketable securities and Accounts Receivables.

### *Forms of Liquidity and Choice of Liquidity*

A company's demand for cash does not always keep the entire amount in the form of cash balance in the current account for the simple reason that the opportunity cost of idle cash is considerably high. That is why, companies try to maintain, besides cash, other liquid assets which provide some return but at the with relatively low risk. Let us first consider the forms of liquidity and then the choice of liquidity mix.

#### *Forms of liquidity*

*Cash Balance in the Current Account:* This is the highest

form of liquid asset a company can conceive of, but the return provided by it is nil. However, companies maintain approximately four to five per cent of their total assets, on the average, in this form despite no returns for reasons already explained.

*Keeping Reserve Drawing Power Under Cash Credit*: This form of liquidity appears to be quite attractive as it can have access to bank borrowing. However, constraints imposed by to be. Close scrutiny of the quarterly budgets of the company by banks and imposition of penal interest of two per cent over and above the normal rate of interest on under- or over—utilisation make this form more tedious and time consuming. However, a built-in cushion may possibly be included while preparing the quarterly budgets and during some periods the full amount may be drawn. The tax benefit on the interest makes effective after - tax - rate to be much less costly, even if part of it is held in the form of idle cash. This not only helps as a liquid source but also helps in obtaining equal or higher limits during the forthcoming year.

*Marketable Securities*: These are short—term securities of government such as treasury bills and other gilt edged securities whose default risk is nil and, for that very reason, the return is low. It is preferable to ensure the maturity structure of these short-term securities with the likely periods of excessive cash drain on the part of the company. Then, the transaction costs can be considerably minimized as early liquidation prior to maturity may result in low return from these assets.

*Investment in Inter-Corporate Deposits*: A company can invest money with other companies in the form of short—term deposits ranging from two or three months to five or six months at remunerative rates. However, these deposits being unsecured in nature, are subject to considerable risk, unless the companies accepting such deposits have excellent antecedents as to their paying habits.

From among the different forms of liquidity available to a company a deliberate choice has to be made in selecting an appropriate mix that suits the liquidity requirements of the company and disposition of its management towards risk.

*Choice of liquidity mix*

The choice of selecting the portfolio of cash and near cash assets also known as the choice of liquidity mix is governed by a variety of factors which are briefly explained below:

*Uncertainty Surrounding Cash Flow Projections:* It is generally said that the only certain factor in the corporate environment is its uncertainty. Even if cash flow projections have been made with the utmost care the general uncertainty can at times make the projections go awry. However the degree of uncertainty is more in certain types of industries than in others. For example general engineering industry is more recession prone than others. Consequently, the onset of recession which was not anticipated may call for a thorough revision of cash flows and policy changes in respect of products plans, dividend payments etc.

Similarly tea plantations can get adversely affected with an untimely hailstorm. Even within the same company which is stable and growing certain types of cash flows, especially collections and payables tend to be more uncertain than others. When the degree of uncertainty is high as evidenced by the sensitivity of cash forecasts to adverse changes in some of the underlying assumptions, the company will do well to have the liquidity mix tilted largely towards cash balance and in so far as possible reserve drawing power under the cash credit / overdraft arrangement and to a less extent gilt—edged securities.

On the other hand certain types of industries such as synthetic fabrics, electrical appliances enjoy stable and growing demand. Once a company has established its image the degree of uncertainty surrounding cash flow projections will be comparatively less. Consequently the liquidity mix of such companies will be tilted more towards marketable securities and inter-corporate deposits.

*Attitude of the Management towards Risk:* When the management of the company attaches greater importance to a given percentage increase in return than to the same percentage increase in liquidity, the portfolio of liquidity mix chosen tends to have a higher proportion of cash balance and marketable securities and cash balances. When the attitude of the management towards risk is quite conservative the liquidity mix chosen tends to have a higher proportion of cash balance and marketable securities and a lower proportion of intercorporate deposits.

*Ability to Raise Non - bank funds:* When a company is favourably placed in a position have ready access to non—bank funds it can afford to have less proportion of cash and more of intercorporate deposits and marketable securities. This kind of a situation arises mostly in the case of group companies. For example, when a manufacturing company promoted by a group faces cash shortage, a Finance and Investment Company promoted by the same group can come to its rescue by providing funds. Such a company need not maintain a large portion of its liquid assets in the form of cash. Similarly, companies, which can control its cash flows effectively, need not hold a large proportion of idle cash in their liquidity mix. This kind of situation can arise in the cash of companies that have horizontal or vertical integration. For example a manufacturing company, which has got substantial interest and / or has promoted another company for the supply of raw materials the company can exercise greater control on payables.

On the other hand, companies which do not enjoy ready access to non—bank sources of funds and / or not in a position to control cash flows may have to have greater proportion of cash and reserve drawing power in their liquidity mix.

# 11

# Impact of Techology in Hotel Business

The financial markets are making massive investments in the companies that deliver Internet technologies, content and related products and services, and the corporate world is now moving toward e-business offerings at a rapid clip.

On the business-to-business (b-to-b) front, e-business is projected to grow enormously in the United States over the next several years, with business-to-consumer (b-to-c) trade not as big, but growing just as fast. The McKenna Group estimates that the b-to-b marketplace could grow in value to US$500 billion in 2003. But those estimates may be low. General Motors Corporation, Ford Motor Company and Daimler Chrysler, for example, have just announced that they plan to combine their efforts to form a b-to-b integrated supplier exchange through a single global portal. Meanwhile, on the retail front, the race is on to win the Internet consumer, whose ranks are growing rapidly.

Traditional retailers have much to be concerned about as retail sales over the Internet skyrocket. And while such activity has yet to grow to the same extent in Europe and Asia/Pacific where the cost of phone calls remains an issue, it surely will over time. In the meantime, travel is one of the more popular online products for sale and over the next several years, it is projected in the United States alone to grow to US$12 billion.

E-business is rewriting the economic rules globally for every industry—including hospitality, travel and leisure. Indeed, it's important to recognise that we are now operating in what has been described as the "new economy," as global trends drive change, including globalisation, consolidation, convergence, technology and communications. Even more, it is clear that the underlying sources of value are also changing. Use of intangible assets such as information, brands, customers, relationships and networks distinguish the most successful companies in the world.

## Impact of the Internet

It is clear that the Internet is having a huge impact on how we conduct our lives and our businesses. And it arrived virtually overnight. In the United States, for example, it took 38 years for television to get into 50 million homes. For the Internet, it took just five years. And for those U.S. consumers that are online, four out of five believe that the Internet is a more important invention than television. Of these same online consumers, close to six in 10 prefer e-mail to paper mail for business correspondence and over one in four check their e-mail while on vacation.

The Internet is also changing the customer relationship—undermining and redirecting customer attention to new sellers of products and services and away from their traditional relationships. And as this occurs, the traditional approaches that hospitality businesses have taken to distribution are all being affected. From reservations taken over the Internet, which are projected to more than double to 9% of volume over the next year, to the declining role of the travel agent.

This occurs as so-called "infomediaries" provide information and access, and software robots troll the activity online to develop matches between buyers and sellers, analysing complex patterns and looking for trends for marketers to capitalise upon. As for the infomediaries, we can expect some of these to move into the transactions business and continue the process of disintermediation. For some hospitality companies, it may be best to join this new competition, particularly if it cannot be beaten at its own game.

The reality today is that the balance of power is shifting from sellers to buyers and in so doing it makes the importance of delivering high-quality service, convenience and value for money ever more compelling. The Internet has clearly leveled the playing field by making price information broadly available to the consumer. Internet business models affect product and services offerings, pricing, distribution and customer service, as well as long-term information capabilities. As a consequence, some hospitality suppliers will inevitably feed different tranches of their inventory through the various channels at their disposal—including the Internet, travel management organisations, destination packagers and the like.

### *Convenience and Consistency for Customers*

In the end, customers want both convenience and consistency. They don't have all the leisure time that futurists once predicted they would have by now. In fact, they have less. Today's fast-paced world produces ever more stress, and consumers want information and they want it fast. And if hospitality companies and travel providers don't deliver convenience, somebody else inevitably will. They also want to be wired up to the rest of the world—at home, in their office and especially when they travel.

And for hoteliers trying to cope with in-room technologies and the delivery of high-speed Internet access, we will soon be seeing more integration of network communication and entertainment products to further complicate or liberate our lives, depending on your point of view. Customers are also looking for consistency—a simple concept, but central to whether a brand has value or not. And in the emerging networked world, aligning the value propositions of alliance partners and ensuring a seamless and consistent experience will only be as good as the weakest link in the chain.

### *New Business Rules*

Within this new economy, the operating environment for hospitality companies is changing. There are new rules of conduct, new relationships and new criteria for success, along with a new set of metrics. The revolution that we must now confront is therefore no less significant than the one that our forebears had to deal with as the Industrial Revolution changed how people lived, worked and dealt with each other. And like our distant relatives of centuries ago, there are boundless opportunities and countless risks, most obscured within an environment of great uncertainty. In such an era there are certain traits to business behaviour that will distinguish success from failure. At this stage in the new economy's evolution, these traits would appear to include speed, agility and flexibility.

Speed is necessary to get to market early with a first-mover advantage that assures early adoption by an increasingly fickle, restless and frequently disloyal customer. Such speed is imperative as so-called "start-up" companies come to dominate their chosen niche in extremely short periods of time, frequently preempting the opportunity for those too slow to react.

Agility is required to be able to respond to competitive threats by not only those we know and can monitor, but also unseen competitors. These latter competitors may not even exist as yet, but as they emerge, they may quickly disintermediate established customer relationships. And, finally, flexibility is needed to reorganise the established models of business and all of the related processes, and adapt the organisation in organic fashion to a new environment in whatever form it takes.

*Human Capital Challenge*

Supporting the changes in the new economy will be a vast pool of talented human capital anxious to bring new ideas and new technologies to bear on the traditional ways of doing business and, in doing so, steadily increase the pace of productivity improvement. And if the hospitality industry is to respond to this coming reality, it will need to address some of its most vexing challenges—particularly those relating to the recruitment, training and development of human capital.

The human capital inventory for an e-business will require entrepreneurship, as well as visionary leadership, strength in sales and marketing and commitment to customer relationship management. The organisational bias will need to be toward creativity and risk-taking, and away from dependency on analysis and procedures.

In addition to the human capital challenge, many of today's legacy organisations are better structured to work in the old economy, but are considerably less aligned for many activities in the "new." The cultural challenges may in fact be no less daunting than those presented by some of the technological ones. For large organisations attempting a major shift in orientation, the presence of a significant culture may turn out to be quite a hindrance.

### *Hospitality Business*

In some industries, profits are made on spare parts and maintenance rather than on mainstream products. In the new economy, we may see this business model replicated in the hospitality industry. And for those companies that discount or give away products such as hotel rooms in order to sell linked services, they surely will be redefining the meaning of hospitality. They will also be marketing an array of hospitality and leisure products and services to a customer base that is no longer satisfied with the traditional ways of making such purchases.

Hospitality businesses that traditionally provided room, board, management and marketing may need to rethink their roles in the new economy, particularly as services become more valuable than products. With the rapid growth of "infomediaries" and their facilitation of transactions, hospitality businesses may need to redefine themselves in order to prosper in an increasingly electronic world where one-to-one customisation is the order of the day. But for those contemplating repositioning their companies in an e-business environment, it will be necessary to focus on the current value proposition of the business and determine how it might be reformatted or enhanced to ensure success in the new setting.

### *Preparation of Global Hospitality Industry*

In Arthur Andersen's recently published global survey of technology, Hospitality 2000: The Technology, we addressed some of the issues that the industry is facing. These included the closed nature of our technology architectures, the way in which we collect information on our customers, our investments in Internet, intranet and extranet technologies, and our adoption of electronic commerce. The results are not especially encouraging and suggest an industry still relatively slow to adapt to e-business.

Only 39% of the industry's Web sites, for example, can handle reservations on a real-time basis, and even fewer still (19%), collect customer information. At the same time, just 22% are using "push" marketing programs and a distinct minority (just 19%), have extranets to suppliers or customers. But these adoption rates are nonetheless projected to grow and we should, therefore, expect our industry's leaders to be far more attuned to the needs of an e-business environment in the years to come.

As information technology (IT) is used to facilitate a company's entry into the world of electronic commerce, our industry's leadership will also need to overcome a natural tendency to be disappointed by the role of IT in achieving competitive advantage. For many years IT was seen as a mechanism to support back office finance and accounting functions.

In the future, it inevitably will be one of the principal drivers of value creation in the new economy. But we should not be mislead by IT—in e-business, it will be the strategy, not the technology that will make the difference between success and failure. But having the strategy in place is only the first step. It must be linked to every part of the business.

### *E-business Planning*

With the costs of playing in the e-business world escalating rapidly, hospitality executives should consider the four phases of what might be called the "E-Business Lifecycle." The first of these—E-Business Strategy Development and Planning—must address the market and competitive context, articulate the vision and opportunity, outline the strategy and the business case, and identify the risks.

In recent years, we have frequently seen hospitality businesses put up a Web site on the Internet and consider this an e-business strategy. But without a strategy for this new form of commerce and the business planning process to drive it, such reactionary approaches stand little chance for success. Once the plan is in place, an e-business design phase can commence to address site design, lay out the business architecture, identify the technical infrastructure, plan for performance, availability and capacity, and deal with tax issues and enterprise security.

Following the design phase, E-Business implementation will prepare for the launch with training and change enablement, implementation and integration, testing and roll-out. Once in place, E-Business Operations will need to be supported by IT and audit services, Web site activity analysis and Web site maintenance. Finally, measurement systems will need to be established to monitor performance. As industry executives embark on this e-business lifecycle, they will need in the first stage to clearly establish the business case for investing in new technologies, systems and organisations by addressing both the cost reduction and revenue enhancement benefits.

On the revenue side, there are a number of factors to consider. These include the company's ability to identify and recruit the most valuable customers; the ability to seamlessly cross-sell the company's products and services, as well as those of alliance partners; the ability to retain valuable customers and reduce attrition; and finally, when and how to eliminate costly and unnecessary discounts through revenue optimisation.

In this kind of environment, the property management system will no longer hold sway as the center of the hospitality universe, but will become just one in a series of customer touch-points that will increasingly include the Internet. These touch-points will ultimately need to be fully integrated into a customer information system supported by sophisticated data warehousing and data mining technologies.

Adding to the industry's costs in this portrait of the future is the cost of grafting e-business technologies onto the industry's legacy systems. At a certain stage, it may make sense to start from scratch and ensure that every system is Web-enabled. This would allow a total interface for a high-growth e-business, thereby maximising the customer relationship management opportunities that it presents.

### *Success on the Internet*

As to the role of the Internet, its comprehensive reach and ubiquitous nature nas already ensured its central place in the new economy. But how should we evaluate whether an Internet application is deserving of our attention? Firstly, productivity on the Internet in the years to come will be vastly improved by much higher bandwidth than is currently in place. And with higher bandwidth will come applications that can benefit from such extra capacity delivering tightly focused and reliable content to an increasingly sophisticated and demanding e-customer. If an Internet application is to succeed in the future, it will therefore need to be designed to capitalise on this coming reality.

Secondly, an Internet application needs to form a community of some sort because without a sense of place, albeit of the virtual sort participants will not have that all-important sense of belonging. And as with the industrial revolution, which drew a disparate population to centers of economic activity, so will such "intranet communities" grow in value as their populations increase in size and their economic product expands.

For larger businesses that form such communities, they are developing new revenue sources and are reinventing their relationships with customers, employees, suppliers and partners. Smaller companies intent on participating in this new environment, may need to be content as a participant in an established community, rather than trying to take on the creation of a community itself. It is better, perhaps, to be one of many players in a successful space than struggling to establish an identity in a world surrounded by also-rans.

Whether large or small, community developers and marketers of the virtual sort will have to recognise that what may have appeared cool in the physical world to generations brought up in the old economy will not work in the world of e-business. Being cool and staying that way in order to get and keep attention will remain a constant challenge, especially for those keen to nurture a younger generation of travelers brought up on MTV and the Web.

Finally, the successful Internet application needs to improve service while reducing transaction costs, particularly as the balance of power in the buy/sell relationship continues its inexorable migration from sellers to buyers. Service improvement strategies will be nothing new for hospitality businesses, but it is noteworthy that service is the top factor that encourages return e-business. This must be an area of focus since the current growth of e-business appears destined to outpace the supporting infrastructure and its related service at least over the short term.

But as hospitality executives know, delivering good service can be expensive. Scaling the types of service response to the circumstances is a growing need, but one that can be modulated if the value of each customer can be distinguished and the response adjusted accordingly.

In considering the opportunities in hospitality e-business, industry leaders should take stock of the dynamics that are occurring in the new economy and plan accordingly. It is probably easy to dismiss the e-business world as a playground for others with products and services that are more obviously applicable. But our industry is changing, as is the world around us. And as alliance partners, vendors, customers, employees and systems all become Web-enabled, hospitality companies must adjust their strategies, organisations, processes and technologies accordingly.

## Challenges Facing the Hospitality Industry

No single factor looms with more uncertainty or greater complexity for investors in the hospitality sector than how the industry can best make technology investments to gain competitive advantage. Technology is a big ticket item in terms of costs, and the amounts investors are being called to finance are growing. And if the industry plans to keep on top of new advances, it will cost even more. Indeed, some hospitality companies have invested unprecedented sums in technology while others continue to face the challenge of persuading hesitant third-party owners of the merits of such investment.

These and other factors pose important questions. If investors do not support spending on technology, hospitality companies will suffer not just in information management but in service to guests. But what price tag for technology is appropriate? Even more, what are the implications for the hospitality industry as technology ultimately creates seamless networks of information and opportunities worldwide? What will this mean for hotel operations, marketing and customer service?

## Hospitality Technology

Today's hospitality industry technology represents a legacy reflecting the computer industry's capabilities during the last two decades and the willingness of hotel executives to embrace its products. We stand the latest wave of a historical evolution beginning with the early hotel accounting systems in the 1960s and early 1970s. These were followed by a variety of front office systems introduced in the 1980s and finally to today's property management systems and the latest efforts in integrated customer information systems, data warehouses and the like.

But in recent years, critics have been increasingly harsh with their comments on the computer systems and software applications used by the hospitality industry. Typically custom-designed for proprietary application, these systems have not always been successfully integrated. In the past hotel owners and management companies would buy products from technology vendors specialising in one area or another and integrate these systems with varying degrees of success.

The hospitality industry is thus beset by a multitude of technology applications offered by numerous hardware and software vendors. There are, for example, no fewer than 85 different property management Systems available to owners and managers of hotels offered by technology purveyors, some stable longterm providers to the industry, others much less so.

Meanwhile, most technology vendors continue to address individual parts of the industry's real needs with little regard to total system solutions. And hospitality companies tend to contribute to a fragmented marketplace quite simply by the way they purchase systems. It is often the case that a hotel company will buy a reservation system from one vendor, a property management system from another and a marketing system from yet another, depending on who makes the best products. And while there are proprietary "clusters" of related technology, the general fragmentation that has existed appears unlikely to change in the near future.

Even more importantly, the industry has failed to cooperate in the development of shared technologies. Moreover, little change in attitude has been evident during the past three or four years as the technology revolution continues to roll forward at an ever-quickening pace. And when a sound system solution is delivered to address an industry need, there is no mechanism for it to become an industry standard and thus picked up by others struggling with the same problem.

With the variety of applications for different parts of the business attended to by different vendors, it is not surprising that interface and integration are now major problem areas to be attended to. What some critics refer to as the industry's problem with closed architecture has undoubtedly cost the hospitality industry money, eroded efficiency and limited technology's benefits.

But the race to put technology to work for the industry also leads to other questions related to global marketing to consumers, as well as the expanding customer services that will ultimately include Internet access and other technology routinely placed in guest rooms. All this, of course, comes at a cost. The choices that hospitality companies make in the technology realm will have profound impact on competitiveness and return to investors. These choices are not easy. Indeed, they may be among the most complex the industry faces.

### *Integrating Disparate Systems*

While integrating disparate systems is an important challenge for the industry, it is fortunately a somewhat easier task today than it has been in the past. Whereas previously hotel computer systems would tend to be free-standing and require modest maintenance, we are now migrating rapidly to environments that include Windows applications and network solutions in which that middle component is becoming a more significant element in the system.

Integration is clearly an important step into the future, with connectivity established between individual property operations, customer information systems, data warehouses and centralised management. The question for many hotel organisations remains how to achieve the ultimate open system that can be shared at all levels, whether it is the central reservation system, individual property management system or any other operational area. Until now, the center of the universe has been the property management system, but that era is ending as companies realise that an exclusive focus on the customer must be supported by fully-integrated customer information systems. Anyone who is arguing on behalf of a closed system in this kind of an environment is arguing against the market.

### *Industry Standards*

Not all the responsibility for integration, however, lies with technology providers. On the buyer's side there must be greater recognition of the commonality of needs regardless of the type of hotel property involved. Is it really necessary to continue to re-invent the wheel, for example, with all of the differing property management systems now available in the market? Even more, can the hospitality industry agree on technology standards, which are essential for full conformance and integration of systems? If the vendors can agree on interfaces between their products and other subsystems, the hospitality industry could benefit greatly.

The lack of industry-wide standards - or a hospitality industry organisation to create or endorse such standards is clearly a stumbling block. There may be some rationale for keeping certain applications proprietary to individual companies and their properties. But falling to support development of shared interfaces between systems is short-sighted at best.

And ultimately it is not the hardware or even the software that delivers the competitive advantage it lies in what management does with the information when it gets it. Note that the successful hospitality organisation of the future is one which reduces the traditional bias towards analysis with an associated increase in creativity. If the industry is to come together and buy into the development of common standards, it will require acknowledgment of this reality.

### *Technology Investments*

Timing is everything in technology investments. For hotel management, knowing when to invest in technology and what new developments to purchase is critical to managing the long-term cost and the benefit of investment in technology. A recent survey suggests that the hospitality industry as a whole has been more conservative than most in making technology investments. Microsoft - in concert with *Lodging Magazine* and *Hospitality and Automation* this year completed an industry-wide survey of technology applications in use and plans for the future.

The survey results revealed that more than 70 percent of respondents are using property management systems word processing spreadsheet, accounting and point-of-sale applications. Fifty percent have sales and catering applications and 20 to 35 percent use presentation programs and scheduling. The Microsoft survey further discovered that 25 to 30 percent of respondents plan to install property management systems, e-mail, sales and catering, point-of-sale and accounting systems in the next 42 months.

On the basis of these results, even the biggest supporter of efforts to systematize our processes would have to acknowledge that this industry remains far behind many others. But with the recent upturn in the industry's fortunes, together with the increased availability of technology at lower per-unit costs than ever before, there are clearly plans to increase spending. The Microsoft-sponsored survey, in fact, went on to discover that 25 to 30 percent of respondents plan to install property management, e-mail, sales and catering, point-of-sale and accounting systems in the next 42 months.

Longer term, 60 to 70 percent plan to install property management, office automation, accounting and sales systems, while 50 percent plan on telecom and food and beverage systems. Forty percent will add in-room applications. Even with these plans, however, there is clearly much to be accomplished in bringing the industry into the next millennium - at least from a technology standpoint.

Technology breakthroughs are generally considered to be cyclical. New applications are coming to market faster than ever before, and the time between conception and implementation grows shorter. It has been said that technology development in the industry once ran in seven-to -nine year cycles. This undoubtedly is no longer the case, however.

In terms of pure technology, recycling appears to be occurring virtually every other year now. For the hospitality industry, the technology development cycle probably breaks into three- to five-year intervals. Indeed, the next breakthroughs in hospitality technology may occur when the property management system is finally dislodged from its place at the center of hotel computer systems. The next big cycle will focus on the fully integrated system that brings customer, statistical and financial information together through an integration of property management, central reservations, data warehouse and distributed database systems. This appears to be where a number of the larger chains already are heading.

### *Use of Network Centric Computing*

We are on the threshold of some major breakthroughs in the use of network centric computing, an expression coined by IBM to describe the remote off-site world of data collection, information processing and system application that occurs in cyberspace.

The integration of computing, telecommunications and interactive cable television to move information is driving this evolution, which will eventually create a seamless bridge for global sources of information. It is only a matter of time until the Internet evolves into a single, powerful highway of information supported by diverse technology applications, many already in development. At the same time, the hospitality industry will also benefit from the development of intranets, internal networks built with the same standards and infrastructure as the Internet and World Wide Web.

Intranets today offer the potential for streamlined and enhanced internal communication, and may be particularly beneficial for large organisations with scattered operations. Further out on the horizon is the prospect of an outsourcing vehicle that can supply the computing service to all-comers, even single hotel property owners who otherwise face a distinct competitive disadvantage as the technology revolution passes them by. And lest the particularly demanding hotel chain be concerned about its unique needs, there should also be the opportunity within an outsourced networked system for appropriate customisation at reasonable cost.

Network computing has enormous implications for marketing to customers on a global basis, as well as hotel operations. Consider the potential for the industry to connect with vendors worldwide for electronic purchasing, potentially achieving economies of scale and leveraging not yet possible. World purchasing functions will allow companies to customise their own catalogs.

Virtual channels of distribution using computer networking capabilities will also allow hotel companies to market products and services - some traditional to our industry, others not - to customers whether they are in the hotel, at work, or at home. This will require a migration from today's central reservation systems to tomorrow's customer information systems using network-centric solutions. Development of customer profiles and guest recognition will make it possible for hotel organisations to interact in entirely new ways with customers, regardless of their physical location.

Clearly, the large hotel companies will need to be the first to address questions raised by global networking capabilities and what this will mean in terms of technology investment. But for many hospitality companies presently struggling with the high cost of technology and the confusing state of our industry's technology affairs, this will not be an easy task. And the decisions will ultimately become further complicated by the opportunity to outsource certain functions into subscription-based networks. It is unlikely that the hospitality industry will be forced to bear the entire burden for networking infrastructure.

Strategic alliances with major technology companies will be the catalysts in building this capability as they become strategic providers of networking capabilities to hospitality and other industries. And as network-centric computing comes of age and a company's proprietary information is stored in cyberspace, security will become an ever-more important issue requiring solutions. Whether it is an e-mail gateway through an internal network or customer access via the Internet, network fire walls and encryption systems will be required to mitigate the concern many will have with system security.

In the final analysis, networking solutions will drive down the cost of technology investment "on-property" where hotel real estate and business interests merge. The solutions that hotel organisations will be able to choose from in terms of networking should also be less expensive than the current profile of technology spending. And we can expect that change to occur sooner rather than later, given the present rate of investment in Internet-based technologies.

### *Technology for Guest*

Meanwhile, the hospitality industry's customers - hotel guests at large -have become increasingly dependent on technology - and more demanding in terms of in-room technology support. This is particularly true for the business traveler whose laptop computer often serves as a mobile office. Technology-driven entertainment options for guests - both business and leisure - also will require investments in the future. Indeed, Internet access will likely be a routine guest service at some point for hotel organisations seeking to remain competitive. And it is hoped we will find inexpensive reengineering solutions that will allow technology to be introduced into physical spaces (such as hotel rooms) without necessitating huge expenditures on rewiring and retooling of existing equipment. The signs of late are encouraging.

Both IBM and Oracle are working on low-end PC products that will provide all of the relevant network interfaces and windowing required. With prices expected in the range of $300 to $700 per device, these appliances will serve an exclusive networking function for economical use in the home. And there are more such products to come as other major technology companies go to market with similar offerings. Clearly, such devices have implications for use in hotel guest rooms.

The industry has historically "mortgaged" its guest room space to third-party providers of entertainment service. In this coming wave of in-room technology, there may be an opportunity for hotel companies to become more proactive in the development and provision of in-room communications and networking solutions that will inevitably need to be provided in the hotel product of the future.

As technology evolves in our industry, we can expect customers to do more and more for themselves. This is already the case with lobby check-in kiosks and use of the Internet as an electronic travel agent to book hotel rooms. Indeed, those capabilities call into question the future of travel agents. What role will travel agents play in the face of increasingly direct customer access to the industry's reservation systems? If your title has the word "agent" in it, it is probably time to be concerned about the tightening of the direct relationship between hospitality companies and their customers, which is now being facilitated by technology.

Ultimately, customers may use Web casting devices that will allow them to create the best itinerary for travel based on a custom-designed profile. The workforce has become increasingly mobile as people work at home and from hotel rooms all over the world. In the future, it is likely that travel related companies will provide booking software modules for use by large corporate customers and individuals alike that will work on home or office computers - with customised profile information that includes hotel and airline preferences or restrictions set by company travel policies. Such a trend will increase the pressure on hospitality companies to respond with sophisticated yield management systems and marketing approaches.

*Maximising Revenue Optimisation*

Yield management - often today referred to as revenue optimisation has come to the hospitality industry via the airline business where high-tech solutions to forecasting based on complex algorithms have generated tremendous improvements in yield. But for yield management to become truly effective in the hospitality industry, much more will need to be accomplished in terms of technology support and the interface between the market reality at the property level and the centralised reservations Systems that have now become such an important part of the industry's distribution system.

Consider what the industry was like before automation. All of the room inventory existed at the individual property level. Over the course of time, hotel companies fractionalised that inventory. Some remained at the property, while other parts moved to a central inventory or out to a global distribution system. Of the various challenges facing hospitality companies in the future, the task of bringing that inventory back to a central location is a significant one.

Such an inventory would produce a single image that can be accessed by all points in the distribution system and would generate consistent information as to availability and pricing - a simple concept with tangible benefits but one that has yet to penetrate this industry. With revenue enhancement opportunities variously estimated in the five- to seven-percent range as such systems are centralised, this should be a quick win for our industry.

### *Telecommunications*

The current state of telecommunications is confusing to most business people in those countries that are privatising and deregulating their telecom industries, In these countries, we can thus assume that the hospitality industry is in a similar state.

The telecom business is in a state of flux worldwide and with deregulation, we can expect more options and competitive pricing. In the United States, for example, it is conceivable that hoteliers will eventually be able to look to one vendor for all telcom needs - local, long distance, 800 number services, cellular, in-room entertainment, data services and Internet access.

In response to this prospect, we are likely to see a greater integration of the computing and telecommunications functions. Voice activation systems will soon arrive in central reservations offices, announcing the beginning of the early breakthroughs in the linking of computing and telecommunications. And as the telecom business continues to privatise and deregulate, the battle for customers will escalate.

Clearly, the industry's leadership will need to keep an eye on this. It will probably take a while for all the dust to settle especially in the United States where there appears to be a free-for-all in this arena. But the end result should be lower unit pricing - an essential element for the hospitality industry as it seeks to align a seamless integration of the telecom and computer systems sides of its business. For international hospitality companies with chains of properties in countries around the world, the outlook should be more circumspect. For such enterprises the delivery of consistent basic telephone service in some countries will clearly need to precede further advancement of telecom technology.

### *Technology Investment*

From a pragmatic view, hotel organisations vary widely in their ability and willingness to track the cycles of technology advances. Some organisations are early-adopters, while others embrace advancements after they have been already tested by others and the investment risk is reduced. Selling the newest technologies outside a small circle of early-adopters in our industry is not easy. And because of the special relationships that exist between hotel companies and the third-party owners of the hotels they operate or between franchisors and their franchisees, selling the technology investment idea to these constituents is also a major challenge.

It is essential that technology investment be sold as part of an integrated business plan where the technology is supporting the plan. In this manner there will generally be greater buy-in from otherwise cynical owners and franchisees who may have other things on their capital spending agenda.

As to the investments required for technology, we can safely predict that there will be significant demands for capital to cover technology investments in the years ahead. The quandary for investors in the hospitality industry, as indeed in many other industries, is how to balance the need to keep up with rapidly evolving technologies with the need for satisfactory returns on capital over the short term. This will require sound planning. Technology investments must support a company's vision and long range strategy.

Given the costs of these investments, no hospitality company can afford to have senior management going in one direction and the information technology function in another. While many companies remain focused on the hardware and software of the technology equation, not to be lost sight of is the critical need for technology leadership either within the organisation or appropriately outsourced by a management team that understands how to manage these processes.

It is also dear that technology planning cannot be cast in stone when new advances are emerging every few months. Historically, the industry has made smaller, one-time investments in technologies. In the future, there will be a need for contingencies allowing for on-going maintenance, support and upgrades. Plans will need to be revisited continually to ensure that sound, on-going investments are made - consistent with an organisation's needs and what is available in the marketplace.

Hotel organisations for years have recognised the importance of reserving capital to replace furniture, fixtures and equipment. A similar approach may prove beneficial in the technology arena. FF&E reserves will begin to share prominence in the financial planning of hotel investments with I.T. (or Information Technology) reserves. Smaller, more frequently planned technology investments should generally pay higher dividends in the long run, as compared to the one-time, major investment followed by years of neglect.

Further complicating the long-range planning for technology investment in an era of network-centric computing is the question of whether to invest in company-based systems or to wait for the availability of network subscription services provided by outside technology utilities. This may still be a long time in coming but given the big numbers involved for large hospitality companies, it is something to keep on the radar screen.

Hotel companies are not in the technology business. But there will clearly be a price for organisations that do not keep up with customer service and operational efficiencies that technology makes possible. That raises significant questions in terms of investments. Stockholders will be called on to spend money on technology, and those investments are critical for hotel organisations not just in terms of the process improvement opportunities but also in terms of service to customers who are, after all, the ultimate arbiters of a company's success or failure.

In the end, however, management will need to understand that technology and information alone confer no competitive advantage. leadership and sound planning will be required to ensure that these investments and the highway of information they generate ultimately produce the shareholder returns required.

## Foundations of the Hospitality

The dawning of the new millennium has seen the very foundations of the hospitality and travel industries shift as major global businesses begin to adopt eBusiness strategies in both business-to-customer (B2C) and business-to-business (B2B) spaces. But are powerful, networked technologies simply an "add on" to the core business of mainstream companies? Or are we witnessing deep changes in the way hospitality and travel businesses organise themselves? We believe the latter is the case as companies redesign their businesses.

Hotel and travel companies have traditionally viewed technology as an enabler. Large-scale technology implementations have generally been part of efforts to design more robust business processes to reduce costs, improve quality and speed time to market. Once the opportunities are identified, teams assess the role that information technology might play in the implementation.

In contrast, Internet technologies are more than enablers in the new economy. They are the drivers of entirely new business models. The successful companies of the 20th century are beginning to understand that the marketplace of the 21st century requires them to acquire and retain a critical mass of valued customers, and they are developing new competencies to deliver new sources of value to these customers. The foundation of success increasingly is the ability to create new business models that leverage Internet technologies to deliver unique value to customers.

### *Diverse Factors*

Diverse factors are driving the successful 20th century businesses in hospitality and travel to reinvent themselves for the 21st century using eBusiness. But the drivers of change differ in Business to Consumer (B2C) and Business-to-Business (B2B) spaces. In the B2C arena, the desire to strengthen customer relationships, develop new revenue streams, enhance profit margins and create more value are all motivating rapid change. The foundation of success increasingly is the ability to create new business models that leverge Internet technologies to deliver unique value to customers.

### *Internet Intermediaries*

Internet intermediaries such as lastminute.com and travelocity.com have recently spent large amounts of marketing funds to build brand awareness. Bass plc and Starwood Hotels & Resorts Worldwide, for example, took early equity stakes in lastminute.com, which sells distressed room, flight and other inventory. The business has moved rapidly and successfully in building high levels of brand awareness out of the starting gate. Loyalty programmes targeting Web-site purchases have now evolved. This new brand awareness and loyalty is a direct threat to the decades of investment in the bricks-and-mortar brands of the industry.

As online clearinghouses (businesses selling distressed room inventory) appeal to a growing number of customers, they are directly challenging the hotel brands. Online purchasers may no longer be buying a Holiday Inn room - rather they may be buying a lastminute.com weekend break or a priceline.com vacation. The major brand owners have had to fight back. And aligning with competitors in the industry is often perceived to add more value than aligning with the new intermediaries.

Customers' needs do not stay the same. The hotel industry meets the core need of providing a safe and secure home-away-from-home for the business and leisure traveller. But an increasing number of guests - business and leisure, domestic and international - require high-speed Internet access and related capabilities. Guests expect remote-office (and entertainment) environments no less functional than they have at home or in the office. Recently, we have witnessed agreements being signed by Windsor Hospitality Group and Four Seasons, Mandarin Oriental (with STSN) and several other chains. Under these agreements, hotels are able to offer their business and leisure clients the same levels of Internet access (speed and response, for example) that has become the norm in their offices or at home.

### *Incremental Revenue Growth*

The new intermediaries have used technology to create other revenue generating tools. There has always been distressed inventory, but networked technologies are allowing the industry to sell it effectively rather than let it perish. There has always been the aspirational non-user of hotel product and services. Now technology is allowing the industry to sell attractively packaged offerings to a market that heretofore has been difficult to identify and reach. Used intelligently, these businesses are adding a further arrow to the marketer's quiver - enabling the industry to add occupancy by targeting specific (and new) market segments.

The extreme last-minute decision-maker and the highly price-sensitive traveller are both in this category. Growing numbers of consumers now compare room facilities and rates, and they are learning to bid for rooms and spare seats on aircraft. A third-party can do the aggregation and the constant updating. It can also act as a brand buffer allowing companies to discount unsold seats or unsold rooms indirectly. The Internet's cost efficiency appeals to companies that currently manage travel offline, and it should lead to an increase in the number of companies that manage travel overall.

We have seen the successful hotel businesses of the old economy partnering to compete with the start-up businesses of the new economy. As these ventures get off the ground, they have the potential to cut deeply into the revenue streams of the new Internet businesses, which have relied on commissions and on the sluggish response to market threats of the airlines and hotel companies. It will not be that easy to get companies with an ethos of confidentiality to cooperate with competitors - in the process promoting transparency to common customers. But by pooling their resources, the major hospitality and travel chains can develop portals quickly and at lower risk to compete in this dynamically changing market.

### *Corporate Policy*

The corporate traveller is a key segment targeted by almost all the major brands. Corporate policy, rather than individual choice, increasingly dictates business travel. According to Forrester Research, Inc., companies eager to save travel and processing costs will mandate the use of Web-based corporate booking engines. The few remaining unmanaged business travellers will buy their business travel online as leisure bookers do.

Corporate policies will increasingly require travellers to use company-approved online booking engines. These engines deliver two elements to improved margins - directed use of a company's negotiated room rates with their preferred suppliers, as well as reduced service charges for making employee travel reservations. Due to the self-service nature of online business travel booking, companies and travel suppliers must increase efforts to encourage continued use.

The Internet's cost efficiency appeals to companies that currently manage travel offline, and it should lead to an increase in the number of companies that manage travel overall. Companies with larger travel budgets can be expected to be the first to shift their travel buying online with 70 percent of Fortune 1,000 companies making this migration by 2002, says Forrester. Larger accounts that are currently unmanaged will increasingly buy online and thus will soon adopt managed travel. Even smaller firms will move their business travel online as well, first encouraging individuals to use any Web interface, then gradually adopting targeted services.

Each managed traveller's company computer will include a desktop icon, which, after entering a user name and password, will link directly to a personalised profile within the travel site. Once business travellers sign on to corporate travel sites, entire trips can be booked with one click on the desktop icon, eliminating the need to re-enter login information. On the road, managed travellers will have the ability to research upcoming trips, check on late flights or change an existing hotel reservation.

### *Loyalty Challenge*

Due to a combination of new bookers and the increasing amounts consumers are spending, the online travel market continues to boom. Travel sites, however, face the same challenges that online retailers struggle with - most consumers are not loyal. Web travellers rely upon the convenience, abundant information and low prices found online, and they are willing to research multiple sites for the best deals.

Forrester divides customers into three segments: disloyal, curious, and loyal bookers. "Disloyal" bookers, customers who research and book at multiple sites, search far and wide to find the best deals for their sophisticated travel needs - including the lowest prices, enticing special offers and exacting itinerary requirements. "Curious" bookers research multiple sites, yet return to the same site to book travel and accommodations.

The third category identified by Forrester, "loyal" customers research and book at one site. Both curious and loyal consumers rely on one site due to easy site navigation, favourable previous experiences and low prices. B2B applications are even bigger accelerators of change than those in the B2C space when it comes to how hospitality and travel companies will do business in the years ahead.

Even though many customers aggressively seek choices to meet their needs, some sites attract more loyalty than others. The one-stop-shop nature of online travel agencies effectively attracts bookers that rely on one site for all their booking needs. Hotel chains, on the other hand, may have a harder time attracting loyal bookers because they are offering only one element of the travel package.

Hotel chain web sites can lure disloyal bookers away from agency and consolidator web sites with special room rates and upgrade perks available exclusively online. Although portals have the greatest reach of all travel sites, they get the lowest percentage of bookers from all three segments. To combat online booker disloyalty, hotels, agencies and portals must take lessons from online retailers on how to encourage loyalty.

Suppliers must establish dynamic partnerships with suppliers in other travel categories that allow consumers to book flights, hotels, and car rentals at the same site. Hotel chains must sell adjacent categories of products and services. Portals should let the agencies and hotels fight over bookers and instead focus on what portals do best - offer information to consumers.

### *Accelerators of Change*

B2B applications are even bigger accelerators of change than those in the B2C space when it comes to how hospitality and travel companies will do business in the years ahead. The B2B space is populated by many types of companies, including links among supply chain partners and market exchanges selling products and services online to businesses. eProcurement is one example of a growing B2B space in the hotel industry. Adoption of B2B strategies that connect businesses in varied ways is being driven by a number of factors:

### *Application Service Provision (ASP) Model*

Yesterday's information technology (IT) model was based on each hotel and/or hotel group maintaining an in-house IT team, which owned and managed the business's hardware and software. Tomorrow, most businesses will have migrated to an Application Service Provision (ASP) model.

Under the ASP model, providers offer a variety of applications and services to companies, which these clients can access with nothing more than an Internet link to the ASP site. This marks a dramatic change from the traditionally defined "service bureau," which once involved the transmission of operational data to an outside agency for management by a remote application. More recently, the explosion of Internet-based software applications and services by ASP providers has caused old economy and new economy businesses alike to revisit off-premises application processing.

The processing of unit-level data at a distant site via an ASP provider may well represent one of the most important ways to obtain mission-critical IT solutions in the hotel industry on a cost-effective basis. Micros-Fidelio, for example, introduced the OPERA ASP application at HITEC. MICROS-Fidelio's Director of Hotel ASP Sales and Solutions, Barry Lowenthal, said: "The marketplace is moving toward seeing the value of ASP solutions. Some chains will do their own hosting, others want services provided."

Serious concerns remain about data ownership and the risk of whether the public Internet offers the speed, data security and reliability to support a highly interactive PMS application. But this is a dynamically changing area, and companies can expect to see ASP technology being introduced to radically simplify IT infrastructures. The ASP model will most likely be successful in the case of vendors offering a complete range of outsourced products - not just a PMS or CRS, but the complete systems operation for properties.

### *Wireless Application Protocol (WAP)*

Mature businesses are not simply assuming that a focus on eBusiness is enough. The wireless market will introduce new competitive elements. Wireless Application Protocol (WAP) is a global specification that gives wireless devices - including mobile phones, personal digital assistants (PDAs) and computer terminals - access to the Internet. The distinguishing feature of wireless service is the ability to identify a user's location.

The network seeks out the mobile phone to complete the call and knows where the holder of the phone actually is. This offers advertisers a dream channel to target customers in a personalised, time- and location-specific way. What are the potential applications or competitive threats? Looking at the customer-facing systems, there is every likelihood that WAP-enabled functionality will be developed to provide access to hotel reservation systems and loyalty traveller databases.

In the administrative areas, WAP technology can be applied to interface the mobile sales force with the centrally held customer relationship management (CRM) database - linking the revenue generating and cost generating systems in the bedroom to the centrally hosted property management system. Realistically, none of this will be available until 2002, but progressive businesses will be determining what strategies to follow, seeking expert advice, and will begin demanding these applications of their vendors as technology progresses and the wireless market, particularly in Europe, develops.

## Mobile Executive in a Global Economy

Globalisation brings new challenges to the hospitality and leisure industries, which are under increasing pressure to serve international business and tourism markets worldwide. Experienced hotel and leisure industry executives have often been transferred outside their home countries, whether to new build locations, new acquisitions or to enhance the provision of services of an existing operation. And in the past, companies often developed compensation packages to attract otherwise reluctant management and staff to accept foreign assignments, the emphasis being on persuading individuals to accept assignments at virtually any price.

With the evolution of a global marketplace, however, attitudes toward assignments out of the home country, as well as provision for compensation and benefits, have shifted significantly in the hospitality and leisure industries. For the truly mobile executive, the strongest development route may now be through a variety of international assignments with that individual bearing some of the "cost" of the assignment in return for stronger career development prospects.

To retain and motivate executives accepting assignments outside the home country, it is important to remunerate them accordingly. Nevertheless, payroll and related costs often account for as much as 45-60 percent of hotel expenses, and it is crucial that the costs of such transfers be controlled. In addition, new and more flexible approaches to compensating those executives accepting overseas assignments are evolving to match the needs of companies and employees in a global economy.

### *Traditional Approach*

The traditional approach to compensating executives transferred from home countries in the past involved a central assumption - executives will be reluctant to take on an overseas assignment, and therefore the process should be as painless as possible. The so-called Balance Sheet approach has broadly aimed to maintain the individual's home country spending power in the new host country.

Once an individual with the requisite expertise was identified and the family/personal issues were resolved, the company developed a package to ensure the individual was not adversely affected financially by the assignment. The individual's basic pay was augmented with additional entitlements or allowances to cover the following:

— Cost of living (COLA);

— Expatriate premium;

— Housing;

— Education (for individuals with families);
— Home leave;
— Professional tax advice; Tax protection/tax equalisation.

When possible and practical, an individual generally continues to pay contributions to social security, pension schemes, and life and medical coverage in the home country. As a result, if the individual is transferred to a country or area with a high cost of living or a more costly taxation regime, providing a remuneration package can prove to be very expensive.

The Balance Sheet approach is relatively easy to understand, reduces suspicion that the executive is being disadvantaged, and by virtue of the fact that the executive is well remunerated, aids mobility. In addition, however, it can be:

— Expensive for the employer;
— Focused on the net benefit to the employee rather than driving down costs for the employer;
— Probably outdated as employers move to a global approach.

*Tax Equalisation and Protection Schemes*

To ensure that the employee is not financially worse off, tax equalisation and protection schemes are often adopted. In a tax equalisation scheme, a hypothetical amount of home country tax is calculated on the usual elements of compensation. The employer withholds the hypothetical tax while paying the actual tax liabilities to the employee's home and host countries. There is often an extra cost associated with this payment of an employee's tax liability by the employer, as this generally creates further taxable income, and therefore there is a tax on tax or 'gross up' effect.

At the end of the year the final hypothetical tax liability is calculated and any under-, or over-payment of hypothetical tax is paid by, or reimbursed to, the employee. Consequently, the executive who has been transferred is no better or worse off than before the assignment. Any benefits arising from tax planning within these schemes are benefits to the company.

With a tax protection scheme the employee is responsible for actual tax and social security liabilities in both the home and overseas countries. These liabilities are then compared to the liability that would have risen had the assignment not taken place and any additional tax costs are reimbursed on a grossed-up basis. As a result, the employee cannot be worse off, but may receive a tax windfall if the actual costs are lower than they would have been in the employee's home country.

### *Net Pay Schemes*

Net pay schemes are also a common feature of such assignments. Hypothetical tax and social security is calculated dependent upon an individual's salary, family size and other factors. The individual's pay, net of this amount, is guaranteed. The employer then assumes responsibility for all actual tax liabilities which are paid on a grossed-up basis. Usually net pay is also augmented by allowances for the individual. An advantage of this method is that no year-end reconciliation is needed as the net pay is guaranteed beforehand.

### *Planning an Assignment*

Tax protection or equalisation in a high tax environment can be very expensive for the employer. Planning an assignment, therefore, is crucial to reducing the associated costs as far as possible. Much can be done to limit the impact of taxes, including:

— Taking advantage of potential tax treaty exemptions. This may require consideration of the number of days spent in the foreign country, and who should be the employer or who should bear the employee's costs.

— Qualifying as a non-resident in years of arrival and departure, and consequently being taxed at a lower rate or not taxed at all. Timing here can be crucial.

— Maximising advantages of graduated tax rates.

— Delivering related allowances as cost effectively as possible. For example, home country social security costs may be saved if a portion of the allowance is paid by the employer as a direct payment to a third party for services such as housing. This is in contrast to providing a cash allowance to the employee, which would be subject to social security contributions.

— Using opportunities such as separate employment arrangements and special premiums for work outside the foreign country.

### *Pension Consideration*

Pensions are another important area for consideration to ensure that pension contributions/coverage are not disrupted. For a short-term assignment an employee generally would continue contributing to his or her home country scheme. However, this may not necessarily be the most tax efficient planning for an individual on a longer term assignment, who possibly may not return to the home country.

A solution adopted in the hotel sector involves establishing a worldwide unapproved plan to prevent employees accumulating limited pension entitlements in several locations. In this case, the benefits of maintaining one single fund outweigh the reduced tax efficiency.

### *Estate Tax Issues*

Inheritance or estate taxes are frequently overlooked when planning an assignment. Generally employers will pay for professional advice in resolving complications with overseas and home country taxes as a result of an employee's death during his or her time away from the home country. This can prove costly to an employer and stressful to the family, so the following should be considered in advance:

— Does a tax treaty exempt the employee from taxes in the host country?

— Has the employee a valid will for both countries?

### *Globalisation*

Globalisation puts considerable pressure on human resource personnel to re-evaluate the traditional methods of providing for executive assignments and to develop innovative new packages suitable for the globalised economy. This represents an increased challenge to human resource personnel during a time when head counts for support functions are under scrutiny.

In addition to the traditional expatriate moving to a specific assignment country and back, typically with a specific technical skill, there is a new breed of mobile executive who has no home country, but rather moves from location to location with career progression a primary motivator. For the latter, a single rigid policy covering different types of employees will be ineffective, and a more flexible, global policy is required.

### *Localisation*

Expatriate assignments also are becoming longer-term because of changes in the business environment. Such expatriates may have adapted to the host country way of life, and as the employer has made the up-front investment in transferring the individual overseas, a solution needs to be identified to phase the individual onto local terms and conditions. The key to a successful transition will be the presentation of the reasons and methodology of the transition policy to the individual in a way which is easily understood and accepted.

### *Balance Sheet Approach*

It is likely that the Balance Sheet approach will soon be outdated as a general method for dealing with international transfers. Despite its popularity, fairness of treatment and logical approach, it is becoming too expensive for the employer to assume tax protection/ equalisation. Furthermore, using general assumptions to calculate the allowances for transferred individuals is often not the most appropriate way to determine benefits. It does not provide an incentive to drive down costs; perhaps most importantly, it lacks the flexibility required in today's global economy to enable the package to be tailored to meet individual circumstance and requirements.

### *Compensation Arrangements*

The move to a global policy for international transfers requires a fundamental re-evaluation of the compensation and benefits approach. Pay and benefits will need to be re-engineered, with a system to differentiate high performance individuals and which reduces the importance placed on the pure money aspects of the pay and benefits package. This is not, however, going to be all bad news for the mobile executive; to date, this individual may not have extracted maximum value out of the assignment package.

The future will see the introduction of more flexible packages of benefits to meet the personal objectives of the individual. Rather than having fixed housing and schooling allowances, for example, an overall price might be put on the remuneration package so the individual can choose how that package is made up and used.

In essence, the individual will be able to pick from a menu of benefits and design the package which is most appropriate to specific needs and aspirations. This menu, of course, must have tax considerations incorporated into the design so that the concept of gain sharing can be used to obtain the employee's buy-in and assistance in developing the benefits which will be offered. Such an approach would be weighted for different assignment locations to take account of local cost differentials.

# 12

# Hospitality E-Business

During the past several years, e-business has changed the business paradigm and has created a new business model across all industries. This new business model is based on creating new channels that facilitate open communication among "service users" and "service providers," enabling information access, information exchange, and procurement of goods and services faster and cheaper. Using this business model, a new breed of young companies have entered the market attracting massive investments and creating extremely high market values.

These new companies have been able to effectively compete with more established and mature companies, taking away their market share, and even acquiring them. Examples of these are AOL acquiring Time Warner, and Travelocity providing air-line and hotel bookings at lower rates than classic travel intermediaries. However, since the new companies have focused on growth and not paid much attention to profitability, their long-term success is questionable, unless they can use the mature company approach of combining growth with profitability.

The emergence of these new e-business organisations has awakened the mature organisations to the need to focus on the e-business paradigm and position their own organisations to benefit from this new business model.

These organisations have realised that if they can be successful in taking advantage of the e-business paradigm, they can regain market share from the new companies because they have the skills and discipline to focus on generating both profit and growth and positioning themselves ahead of their new competition.

## E-Strategy and Plan

The hospitality industry is a prime candidate for benefiting immensely from e-business. In the more distant past, the hospitality industry had been a technology leader with its comprehensive reservation systems and property management systems. Unfortunately during the past decade, this industry has not placed as much emphasis on technology as a critical factor for its future, as it did in the past. However, this industry can no longer lag behind with its technology usage. Now is the time for the hospitality industry to bridge the gap in its technology usage and embrace the Internet and e-business.

The hospitality industry has the benefit of learning from other industries' successes, as well as mistakes, and approach e-commerce with a solid e-strategy to avoid potential pitfalls that its predecessors faced. Currently, most hospitality executives are aware of the impact of this new business model and are actively searching to find ways of incorporating e-business into their companies' operations. However, often these efforts are done reactively and without a clear strategy and plan. While this reactive approach can produce short-term benefits, it will be less effective and more expensive in the long run.

Therefore, to truly benefit from the impact of e-business, it is imperative to develop a clear strategy and roadmap that addresses all aspects of e-commerce. The market leaders are those companies that have a clear vision of how their organisation will benefit from e-business, supported with a comprehensive strategy and plan. A key critical success factor for e-business is having a viable e-business strategy and plan.

There are several steps for hotel companies to consider in developing an effective e-strategy, depending on what their focus is and whether it is mainly directed to identifying and defining new markets and business opportunities or looking to e-commerce to improve the operating fundamentals of the organisation. There are a number of steps typically involved in developing an e-business strategy. Which steps to begin with depend on the focus of the initiatives. A suggested stepped approach to developing an e-business vision, strategy, and plan follows.

*Stage One*: E-Strategy and Branding — Thé first stage in developing the e-business strategy involves determining the e-business readiness of the company and preparing a high-level vision and strategy. Typical steps are as follows:

- Conduct a Net Readiness Assessment — This entails a functional and technical assessment of the company's abilities to develop and deploy Internet applications in support of stated business objectives.
- Prepare a High-Level Business Strategy — A plan should be developed for using the Internet for competitive advantage and growth based on the business's goals, objectives, competitive environment, and culture. Key components typically include:
  - Strategic goals and objectives and corresponding metrics
  - Business vision
  - Identified e-business opportunities and threats
  - High-level initiatives definition
  - Top-level roadmap and timeline
  - Organisational roles and responsibilities

— Develop a High-Level System and Component Architecture — The end-state technical vision should be developed, including cornerstone application system descriptions, proposed technical components including Web and hardware server specifications, high-level network architecture, and integration approaches.

— Refine the Brand Strategy and Positioning — A strategy for managing the company's brands via Internet-based solutions should be developed.

— Develop a Comprehensive Business Case — At this point it is important to develop a business case for all opportunities identified in the business strategy. The business case may document estimates of market valuation or response to e-business initiatives, in addition to classic return-on-investment model parameters and metrics.

— Prepare Prototype Designs — It is useful to develop a prototype to demonstrate functionality and reactive direction based on identified strategic objectives to illustrate the opportunity and create momentum around the chosen initiatives.

— Develop a Go-To-Market Strategy — A need exists to prepare a high-level, go-to-market strategy for the e-business solutions in response to the results of customer needs and customer value assessments.

— Prepare a Detailed Requirements Analysis — This involves defining the functional and technical requirements of the pro-posed business solutions.

— Develop Appropriate Solution Design Specifications — Design specifications should be prepared to reflect the creative and interactive designs developed to meet the business requirements and support the brand positioning.

— Refine Applications, Technical, and Content Architectures — The e-business strategy should contain a description of the underlying application integration framework and development approach, such as EJB or CORBA, as well as the major functional systems within the e-business application solution, hardware specifications, network architecture, and content specifications.

— Develop e-Business Process Specifications and Organisational Design — Business processes for the new e-business model and the changes required to current processes to migrate to the new model should be identified, as well as the new e-business organisational structure for the company or venture.

— Determine the Hardware/ Network Infrastructure — The physical infrastructure that comprises the production and development environments and their opera-tins should be developed.

All of these steps are the basis for an appropriated, staged, designed, and implemented e-business strategy.

## E-business Focus for Hotel Companies

While some hotel companies are successfully entering the e-procurement business and others employ Web-based reservations networks, the industry as a whole is not yet where it should be when compared to other industries. E-business is quickly spreading throughout all aspects of the business. Some of the priorities are briefly described.

In the guest room, for example, guests in some hotels can use the Internet to do a variety of things: access entertainment, shop, plan tours, make reservations, and plan further travel. Several hotel companies, for instance, Hilton.com, are extending their reach to offer services and purchase options to customers outside the hotel environment through their commercial Web sites and Customer Loyalty Program.

As hotel customers increasingly adopt a self-serve view of the world, those properties and chains that capitalise on this trend will be able to differentiate themselves from the competition and gain market share. Wireless applications relating to customer self-service are addressed in another section of this publication. E-business initiatives are underway to connect with and service corporate accounts as well, with proprietary Web-based programs and services and on-line bookings of meetings and catering events.

Another area with potential is the use of the Internet to facilitate hotel back-office functions. The financial, human resources, asset management, and other back-office needs can be effectively addressed through this new channel. Back-office managers, by out-sourcing IT infrastructure and business applications management, may no longer have to worry about maintaining their own systems or having the right technical people to sup-port them. They can "have their cake and eat it too." They can have access to what applications they need through the Internet, when and where they need it. They can focus on their core competency and be business managers who can get the data that they need to manage their operations effectively and turn their organisations into effective and profitable entities.

### *E-Integration*

Hotel companies generally have disparate systems that support individual needs, such as reservation, property management, revenue management, financial management, human resources, payroll, sales and catering, marketing, and many more. Each of these systems is very vital to the operations of the hotel. Each hotel application stores and produces valuable data that needs to be transformed into information that various resources throughout the organisation can access and use to perform their jobs more effectively.

Having consistent, accurate, and timely information can position a hotel with the information that it needs to manage itself more effectively and produce results that can increase revenue, control and reduce expenses, and finally increase profits. The Internet can serve the vital purpose of providing a foundation for integration of various systems and business applications across a wide spectrum of business constituents, including hotel companies, their franchisees, corporate customers, and dispersed business units. This is accomplished by deploying middleware solutions to link legacy back-end business applications to Web front-end applications.

### *Data Integration*

The need to have access to the right data to manage the hotel operations is compounded for the owners of properties with multiple hotel chain affiliations. Since they use different chains' systems, being able to roll up their performance data into a single database that can be used for management and reporting purposes across all properties and chains becomes a significant critical success factor. The ultimate questions for any hotel owner or operator is how to get good customer data and how to store it in a proper repository so it can be utilised as needed.

Many organisations can gather data, but don't know how to consolidate it by different names or variations, such as Bill Smith, William Smith, or W. Smith. Furthermore, a long-standing challenge is to be able to determine who are a hotel's best customers and subsequently tailor specific services for them. For many companies, this is still an impossibility. However, in this day and age and with the new tools available in the marketplace, this should become a reality. In order to achieve the out-lined objectives of integrating data across a company or portfolio of properties, hotel companies need to integrate the data from these disparate systems, maintain the data in a single data repository, provide tools that transform the data into information, and facilitate access to the right data at the right time from any location within the hotel company.

A good vehicle to access the data from any location is the Internet or the World Wide Web. There are new tools that help with data integration, transformation, analytics, and Internet-based access. Using these tools, coupled with a thin client application, staff managers and headquarter personnel can access the right level of data that is pertinent to their need from any location. By using this approach, the dream of knowing who are the right customers can, and will, become a reality.

Having an integrated environment, coupled with an integrated database, can help achieve another long-standing hospitality dream. The dream is to have a single image inventory system where the total room inventory for any major hotel entity is maintained in one place, and all reservation sources access the same database to book rooms. The value of the single image inventory system is in eliminating all unnecessary intermediary reservation steps, thus avoiding over and under bookings. Although many claim to have this capability, it is not yet widely available.

The first organisation that can fully achieve this capability will enter a new era in reservations and will be able to achieve tremendous success. A number of e-business initiatives are under way to de-couple rooms inventory management from PMS applications and distribute reservation data and information over the Web from centrally hosted applications. A number of Web-based reservation services, like Worldres.com and others, are providing fully Web-based solutions for hotels.

### *Hotel Chain Extranets*

The industry needs an effective Web portal, perhaps on a chainwide or even an industry wide basis, that provides operators and owners with information, tools, business applications, and industry best practices to help them run their businesses. Topics could range from labour issues, including how to hire the best people, what incentives to offer to properties for sale, the availability of service companies, and many other functions.

A number of hotel chains, such as Cendant, Choice, and others, have established extranet information portals to push vital information and business tools out to franchisees. A number of hospitality industry vertical Web portals, such as VerticalNet's hospitality portal, have also been introduced recently to offer similar capabilities and information to independent hotels.

### *E-Procurement*

E-procurement as a viable business-to-business Internet solution has taken hold in a major way in the hospitality industry. One major e-procurement consortia, Avendra, involves a joint venture between Bass Hotels, Marriott International, Hyatt, and Club Corp. These companies have pooled their buying power and are in the process of implementing an integrated catalog ordering system linking a variety of suppliers to their hotels and clubs. This is in an effort to dramatically stream-line the purchasing process. Other competing e-procurement exchanges, including Zoho.com, Purchase Pro.com, and H-Suppy.com, are also gaining significant traction within the hotel industry.

## NEW BUSINESS RULES

Within this new economy, the operating environment for hospitality companies is changing. There are new rules of conduct, new relationships and new criteria for success, along with a new set of metrics. The revolution that we must now confront is therefore no less significant than the one that our forebears had to deal with as the Industrial Revolution changed how people lived, worked and dealt with each other. And like our distant relatives of centuries ago, there are boundless opportunities and countless risks, most obscured within an environment of great uncertainty. In such an era there are certain traits to business behaviour that will distinguish success from failure. At this stage in the new economy's evolution, these traits would appear to include speed, agility and flexibility.

Speed is necessary to get to market early with a first-mover advantage that assures early adoption by an increasingly fickle, restless and frequently disloyal customer. Such speed is imperative as so-called "start-up" companies come to dominate their chosen niche in extremely short periods of time, frequently preempting the opportunity for those too slow to react.

Agility is required to be able to respond to competitive threats by not only those we know and can monitor, but also unseen competitors. These latter competitors may not even exist as yet, but as they emerge, they may quickly disintermediate established customer relationships. And, finally, flexibility is needed to reorganise the established models of business and all of the related processes, and adapt the organisation in organic fashion to a new environment in whatever form it takes.

For business executives at large, one of the most compelling changes that has confronted them in recent years is the potential for e-business. But while the significance of these new media are all too apparent, the business solutions required to capitalise on opportunities they offer are unfortunately not. For most hospitality executives, the essential frame of reference has been a geocentric one where real estate and geography have been the big drivers in a physical world—buildings, dots on maps, markets served, chains.

In tomorrow's world, these concepts will require some fundamental adjustments to provide for market "spaces" rather than "places" as the nature of relationships between hotel businesses, their customers, their suppliers and their alliance partners go through rapid and constant change. As these changes occur, the new economy's business leaders must quickly learn the new rules of the game and adjust their approaches accordingly. And the most successful among us will align key processes around the Internet, build corporate intelligence automatically, create integrated value chains and develop new processes to deal with an ever-changing set of circumstances.

### *Human Capital Challenge*

Supporting the changes in the new economy will be a vast pool of talented human capital anxious to bring new ideas and new technologies to bear on the traditional ways of doing business and, in doing so, steadily increase the pace of productivity improvement. And if the hospitality industry is to respond to this coming reality, it will need to address some of its most vexing challenges—particularly those relating to the recruitment, training and development of human capital.

The human capital inventory for an e-business will require entrepreneurship, as well as visionary leadership, strength in sales and marketing and commitment to customer relationship management. The organisational bias will need to be toward creativity and risk-taking, and away from dependency on analysis and procedures. In addition to the human capital challenge, many of today's legacy organisations are better structured to work in the old economy, but are considerably less aligned for many activities in the "new." The cultural challenges may in fact be no less daunting than those presented by some of the technological ones. For large organisations attempting a major shift in orientation, the presence of a significant culture may turn out to be quite a hindrance.

### *Hospitality Business*

In some industries, profits are made on spare parts and maintenance rather than on mainstream products. In the new economy, we may see this business model replicated in the hospitality industry. And for those companies that discount or give away products such as hotel rooms in order to sell linked services, they surely will be redefining the meaning of hospitality. They will also be marketing an array of hospitality and leisure products and services to a customer base that is no longer satisfied with the traditional ways of making such purchases.

Hospitality businesses that traditionally provided room, board, management and marketing may need to rethink their roles in the new economy, particularly as services become more valuable than products. With the rapid growth of "infomediaries" and their facilitation of transactions, hospitality businesses may need to redefine themselves in order to prosper in an increasingly electronic world where one-to-one customisation is the order of the day. But for those contemplating repositioning their companies in an e-business environment, it will be necessary to focus on the current value proposition of the business and determine how it might be reformatted or enhanced to ensure success in the new setting.

But just how prepared is the global hospitality industry to capitalise on some of the opportunities afforded by the emerging new economy? In Arthur Andersen's recently published global survey of technology, Hospitality 2000: The Technology, we addressed some of the issues that the industry is facing. These included the closed nature of our technology architectures, the way in which we collect information on our customers, our investments in Internet, intranet and extranet technologies, and our adoption of electronic commerce.

The results are not especially encouraging and suggest an industry still relatively slow to adapt to e-business. Only 39% of the industry's Web sites, for example, can handle reservations on a real-time basis, and even fewer still (19%), collect customer information. At the same time, just 22% are using "push" marketing programs and a distinct minority (just 19%), have extranets to suppliers or customers. But these adoption rates are nonetheless projected to grow and we should, therefore, expect our industry's leaders to be far more attuned to the needs of an e-business environment in the years to come.

As information technology (IT) is used to facilitate a company's entry into the world of electronic commerce, our industry's leadership will also need to overcome a natural tendency to be disappointed by the role of IT in achieving competitive advantage. For many years IT was seen as a mechanism to support back office finance and accounting functions. In the future, it inevitably will be one of the principal drivers of value creation in the new economy. But we should not be mislead by IT—in e-business, it will be the strategy, not the technology that will make the difference between success and failure. But having the strategy in place is only the first step. It must be linked to every part of the business.

### E-business Planning

With the costs of playing in the e-business world escalating rapidly, hospitality executives should consider the four phases of what might be called the "E-Business Lifecycle." The first of these—E-Business Strategy Development and Planning—must address the market and competitive context, articulate the vision and opportunity, outline the strategy and the business case, and identify the risks.

In recent years, we have frequently seen hospitality businesses put up a Web site on the Internet and consider this an e-business strategy. But without a strategy for this new form of commerce and the business planning process to drive it, such reactionary approaches stand little chance for success. Once the plan is in place, an e-business design phase can commence to address site design, lay out the business architecture, identify the technical infrastructure, plan for performance, availability and capacity, and deal with tax issues and enterprise security.

Following the design phase, E-Business implementation will prepare for the launch with training and change enablement, implementation and integration, testing and roll-out. Once in place, E-Business Operations will need to be supported by IT and audit services, Web site activity analysis and Web site maintenance. Finally, measurement systems will need to be established to monitor performance. As industry executives embark on this e-business lifecycle, they will need in the first stage to clearly establish the business case for investing in new technologies, systems and organisations by addressing both the cost reduction and revenue enhancement benefits.

On the revenue side, there are a number of factors to consider. These include the company's ability to identify and recruit the most valuable customers; the ability to seamlessly cross-sell the company's products and services, as well as those of alliance partners; the ability to retain valuable customers and reduce attrition; and finally, when and how to eliminate costly and unnecessary discounts through revenue optimisation.

In this kind of environment, the property management system will no longer hold sway as the center of the hospitality universe, but will become just one in a series of customer touch-points that will increasingly include the Internet. These touch-points will ultimately need to be fully integrated into a customer information system supported by sophisticated data warehousing and data mining technologies. Adding to the industry's costs in this portrait of the future is the cost of grafting e-business technologies onto the industry's legacy systems. At a certain stage, it may make sense to start from scratch and ensure that every system is Web-enabled. This would allow a total interface for a high-growth e-business, thereby maximising the customer relationship management opportunities that it presents.

## Web Based Marketing

Hensdill describes the Web as "a perfect medium for selling travel". According to Hotel's 1998 Worldwide Technology Survey, 81% of hoteliers worldwide were thought to be capable to accept reservations over the Web in 1999. There is now widespread acceptance of the use of the Web for electronic commerce. The Web's potential as a low-cost distribution channel is having a profound effect on both business and consumers. There are a number of reasons for this. The costs for establishing and hosting a Web site vary greatly depending upon the scope of the project, but can be relatively low.

The Web offers the possibility of high-speed global information transfer, high levels of interaction and links to computerised reservation and database systems, irrespective of geography, time zone, or computer system. There are therefore benefits in extending the firm's marketing reach to the global marketplace; supplanting traditional distribution channels, and allowing potential consumers browsing time by use of Web technology.

The above features of the Web are a possibility for all hoteliers and therefore the Web has the ability to provide equality of access and strategy for all. In addition for larger companies the Web offers a competitive alternative to more traditional computerised distribution channels, such as the Global Distribution Systems. The hotel industry is information-intensive and the Internet is, first and foremost, an information resource. Internet multimedia technology allows for the transmission of sophisticated digital images, video and sound.

Hotel "electronic brochures" can now include moving, three-dimensional pictures of the property and facilities, which the potential customer could explore continuously. Virtual hotel tours can now be found on a number of hotels Web sites and views from selected rooms could be simulated. Ticketmaster Online uses such innovation to provide a unique service that shows the view its customers can expect from their theatre seats, fostering one-to-one relationships with customers.

From the marketing perspective a major benefit of the Web is the greater degree of interactivity than other communication media. The most valuable Web applications are those that allow companies to transcend communication barriers and establish dialogue directly with customers. For example, hotel Web sites can contain electronic forms for customer completion and hotels can reply directly via electronic mail (e-mail). This kind of connection will improve customer relations and contribute towards the building of customer loyalty.

The Web can give access to a greater store of information than other traditional communication media, and provide visitors with the means to select and retrieve only that which appeals to them. This means that customised brochures, itineraries and guides could be produced at the touch of a key. For the hotels, it provides a useful tool in their adoption of micro marketing in this

"Age of the Individual" and relationship marketing. However, it must be remembered that the true determinant is the capability and willingness of customers to use the Web to book hotel rooms and to search for hotel information.

## Relationship Marketing

A new form of marketing has emerged as relationship marketing. Various other terms have been used either as substitutes for RM or to describe some close parallel—micro-marketing, loyalty marketing, one-to-one marketing, wrap-around marketing, customer partnering, symbiotic marketing and interactive marketing. Gummesson supports the view that RM represents a "new marketing paradigm" and the beginnings of a new theory. Evans and Laskin suggest: "RM is a customer centered approach whereby a firm seeks long-term business relations with prospective and existing customers". Similarly, Brodie, and Coviello et al have described the major changes taking place in the continuing transition to relationship marketing.

Some critics of RM suggest that it is really no more than a series of transactions over time. Strong rebuttal comes from Czepiel, who argues that a relationship possesses "mutual recognition of some special status between exchange partners". Barnes adds to this by saying that "a succession of interactions does not necessarily lead to a relationship any more than repeat purchasing constitutes loyalty". True marketing relationships, like other human relationships, should be characterised by the deeper feelings of trust, concern and commitment.

In the current competitive market place hotel companies have found it necessary to win the loyalty of the reduced number of customers. As such they need to reorient their thinking away from merely attracting customers to retaining customers. This is due to the need to reduce the cost acquiring customers as indicated by Rosenberg and Czepiel, Barnes and Cumby, and Liswood. Buttle notes that there are the direct costs of the successful conversion of prospect into a customer as well as the costs of unsuccessful prospecting. Thus, keeping customers loyal is a sensible business strategy.

Even with successful campaigns, companies still face the risk of customers defecting, i.e. stop coming back. Defection rates affect retention rates, which is a central issue in relationship marketing. Price Waterhouse calculated that a 2% increase in customer retention is equivalent to a 10% reduction in costs. There is growing awareness of the lifetime value of customers. A transaction-orientated view of the customer would consider the sales value and margin earned from a single sale, while a relationship-orientated view considers the revenue and contributions earned from a long-term relationship with a customer.

Gilbert argues that the lifetime value of retaining customers enables the costs of conversion of the prospect to be set against the revenues earned over the long term. Sales and profits will also improve in direct proportion to the length of time a relationship lasts. In addition, existing customers tend to make more frequent visits, may broaden the base of their own purchases over time, and influence others through word-of-mouth advertising.

A relationship marketing paradigm is most suitable when:

— there is an ongoing or periodic desire for service on the part of the customer;

— the service customer controls the selection the service supplier;

— there exists alternative choice of suppliers;

— word-of-mouth is an especially potent form communication about a product;
— brand switching is a common phenomenon;
— there is an ability to cross sell products.

These characteristics are typical of the hotel industry. RM can also be considered as particularly suitable for the hotel industry because of the ease with which the industry can adopt it. Hotels already possess important customer data from accommodation bookings and the registration process. It is also possible for hotels to retrieve other valuable information from hotel records, such as frequency of stay and spending behaviour. This data can be organised in a database system and manipulated to identify and target customers directly. Hotels are then in an ideal position to begin a relationship with customers.

## Hotel and Tourism Marketing

The objective of relationship marketing is customer retention. Various hotel and tourism marketing academics have proposed alternative strategies for achieving it. Gilbert proposed that the long-term retention of customers requires the following five steps:

1. *Identify more about the customer through database analysis*: The role of the hotel Web site would be to compile information on an individual's purchases or desires, using an incentivised on-line questionnaire. The Web could also track and measure customers reactions to different offers posted on the hotel Web site. Customer profiles could then be created.
2. *Improve and make the product/service more attractive*: Again, customised on-line questionnaires could be targeted to frequent guests to collect their attitudes to services or loyalty programmes. The hotel company could use this information to improve aspects of the

service that are not meeting or exceeding the expectation of customers. In addition, lapsed or inactive hotel customers could be cost-efficiently contacted using e-mail.

3. *Inform to build customer's knowledge of the company*: The Web could serve as a strategic information centre. Key information, such as lists and locations of key agents, as well as hotel company updates on new products, services, offers and benefits, could all be posted on the hotel Web site. Electronic newsletters could also be e-mailed to both prospective and loyal customers. In this mariner, customers will have increased knowledge of the hotel company, which could enhance customer brand loyalty.
4. *Tempt customers to purchase more regularly, try different products, etc.*: The Web could be used to implement this objective by the direct c-mailing of special electronic promotion leaflets to frequent hotel guests. Furthermore, the hotel Web site could be designed to cross-sell other hotel products/services. For example the Hilton Hotels & Resorts Web site has an "electronic hotel concierge" who tempts customers to try other services of Hilton by displaying short messages.
5. *Retain the customer by developing different forms of loyalty schemes*: Inspired by the success of the airlines' frequent-flier programmes, hotels have started their own frequent-stayer programmes or customer loyalty schemes. A Web site could be designed for the exclusive use of hotel loyalty scheme members. Entry into the Web site is restricted through the use of identification numbers and passwords. Member's only magazines and special offers could be posted on these exclusive Web pages. Various customer services could also be offered, again exclusively to members. For example, the members of Sheraton's loyalty

programme, Sheraton Club International, can keep track of their account activity and redeem rewards on-line.

Gilbert's model can also be considered within the context of criteria for a successful Web strategy advocated by the Butler Group, which advises organisations to:

— treat the Internet as a new medium and exploit its unique properties, such as interaction with customers;
— start with customers by defining who they are and what they want to know;
— build relationships with customers by getting to know them, customising content for them and ensuring relevance to them;
— build a service, not a Web site by giving customers value for time and money and by providing options not available elsewhere;
— leverage existing business by building on assets (brand names, operational infrastructure, information, customer relationships); and
— think radically to achieve the best chance of obtaining the benefits offered by the technology.

## Characteristics of Web's Multimedia

The Web offers an alternative, single tool as an integrated communication medium. There is general awareness and understanding of the marketing value of the Web's interactive characteristics, but the effects of multimedia attributes remain under researched. Furthermore, the problems associated with bandwidth and slow delivery are additional inhibitors to the wide-scale application of multimedia. However, some researchers advocate its use. Condon suggests that the use of multimedia on the Web home page is able to upgrade the product or service image and facilitate sales.

It is likely that future compression technology and network infrastructure will provide a platform capable of rapid delivery of full media Web sites. It is also reasonable to suggest that multimedia could be used to foster a high involvement condition in hotel customers, encouraging transaction involvement and repeat Web site visits. It is therefore a matter of importance that the hotel industry considers the effect of Web style, particularly in the domain of sound, video and animation. The hotel industry is information-intensive and the sheer volume of information available will become an increasing burden to consumers.

## Research Results of Hotel Web Sites

A major survey of hotel Web sites was undertaken during May 1997 and repeated in November 1999. The sampling frame for the current study can be defined as any hotel group accessible via the Yahoo web site in November 1999. The sampling frame introduces the same bias as in the earlier study, i.e. hotel groups not listed on the Yahoo site are excluded. A total of 140 hotel Web sites were accessed from the Yahoo search engin. The data were recorded against the same checklist used in the original study. Additional Web mechanisms were recorded, as was all use of multimedia by the hotels. Hence every Web mechanism utilised by hotel Web sites in the sample, at the time of the survey, has been listed and analysed.

The data was analysed using SPSS for Windows. Descriptive statistics were used to compute the relative frequency distributions of all variables. The Web research identified the current use of the following web mechanisms:

— information,

— reservation,

— loyalty programme,
— newsletter,
— special gestures,
— feedback,
— customer service,
— public relations,
— value-added services,
— employee web site,
— channel member web site, and
— customised research.

In addition, the research identified the current level of the application of animation and sound in hotel Web sites.

*Information*: The Web is potentially a strategic information centre for the hotel industry, capable of offering the following features: electronic brochure, corporate information, press releases, financial reports, company history, company milestones, product and service information), on-line directory (a listing of hotel properties available which is often categorised by geographical location), property information (facilities available, amenities, transportation services, attractions, travel directions, etc.), what's new, virtual hotel tour as an experience of 'walking through' the hotel property, special promotions and language localisation selection by browser.

The most significant change since the first survey is the nature of the hotel Web sites. They are now providing detailed descriptions and images of most hotel facilities and can therefore be described as electronic brochures. The range and complexity of information now provided by the majority of hotels is evident from the chart above, which shows significant growth in almost all areas of information provision. The only reduction is in the provision of language localisation.

The earlier study revealed slightly more than 35% of hotels providing four or more features utilising the checklist from the earlier model. Again, the growth is significant, with 71% of those surveyed now providing six or more such features. Thus, it is evident that the majority of the hotel chains are exploiting the potential of the Web as a strategic information centre. The authors believe that agent technology could provide a solution for the monitoring and maintenance of a hotel Web site. The ability of agents to operate in a flexible, proactive manner suggests that agent-based systems could be built to monitor changes in both customer behaviour and the outside environment, and equipped with this information, to update previously defined goals.

The agent could then respond by taking the appropriate actions to meet these new goals. This could be the generation of a new, customised Web page for a specific customer group, whose interests have changed or for whom there is new information. Similar applications have already been built. The Zuno Digital Library uses agents in three roles, which represent the consumer, the producer and the facilitator (mapping between consumer and producer). The system retains models of consumers. It then operates in a proactive way by providing information they require and shielding them from information that is irrelevant. The output is not a Web page but the conceptual logic is the same.

*Reservation*: The Web offers the hotel industry a distribution channel that enables customers world wide to book hotel rooms. Internet-enabled distribution strategy has been heralded as a way for small and medium sized companies to compete more equally with larger organisations. The web hotel reservation capability currently includes the following features:

— on-line search,

— on-line availability check,

— on-line reservation form,
— on-line reservation retrieval,
— on-line cancellation,
— real-time processing,
— create/modify profile, and
— e-mail reservation.

The majority of hotel chains are now taking advantage of the Web as a reservation medium. The current survey has revealed growth in all areas of Web reservation for hotel products. Significantly there are more than three times as many hotel chains now offering on-line search facilities and real-time processing as in May 1997.

In line with many other industries, the hotel customer is now taking an active role in the purchase process. A survey by HIMG has shown that business travellers have expressed a strong interest in booking hotel rooms via the Web, and the hotel industry has responded to the changing trends in consumer behaviour. However, there are implications for intermediaries in the hospitality industry, and future roles may be uncertain.

The number of hotel chains using the Web as a strategic extension to their customer databases has doubled from just over 2% to 5%. It seems, therefore, that the hotel industry remains cautious in this area. This may be attributed to the security issues inherent in allowing customers access to critical data.

*Loyalty Programs*: Hotel chains are extending their loyalty programmes on-line by having special features for their potential and existing frequent guests; such as general information, on-line enrolment, restricted frequent guest area, on-line account review, create/modify customer profile, exclusive e-mail address, special Web offers, and request rewards on-line.

The previous study revealed that a high proportion (75%) of the hotel chains offered no loyalty programme features at all. There is significant change in this area, with 45% of hotel chains now offering loyalty features. The growth to 42% of those surveyed offering on-line enrolment is further evidence of the benefits of the interactive nature of the Web. Again, customer involvement is fostered. The number of hotel Web sites offering a restricted frequent guest area has risen to 30%, a clear indication that hotels are recognising the benefits of customer loyalty.

Significantly, hotels seem to be more willing to give loyalty programme members access to customer databases, with 7% of those surveyed allowing such customers the opportunity to create and modify their own profiles, and 8% providing on-line account view. Interesting new research by Palmer et al has identified that while some medium to large-sized hotel groups are investing in collecting customer information, by means of loyalty schemes, they are not making sufficient use of the data.

*Newsletter*: Hotel chains can keep their customers and employees up-to-date with the latest developments using electronic newsletters, which are of two types—Web newsletter and e-mail newsletter.

The growth to 50% in on-line newsletters is in line with the overall trend in on-line provision of services by hotel Web sites. The reduction in e-mail newsletters is significant and may be an indication of the increasing costs in providing such a service.

*Special Gestures*: The Web offers hotel chains the ability to personalise the experiences of customers who visit the Web sites. Hotel chains could include features such as the set up of a personal Web page, address Web visitor by name, welcome message, and guest book. The potential of the Web to personalise customers' on-line experiences remains largely untapped by the hotel chains. The most commonly offered feature is the guest book, with 4% of hotel chains in the survey offering this feature.

*Feedback*: Hotel chains can employ the Web as an interactive marketing tool. Customers could give direct feedback via the Web. This could be done by filling up an on-line form or by e-mailing their comments, complaints or suggestions. This is the only area showing a reduction in provision. Fewer hotel chains than in May 1997 offer either feedback mechanism. This may be explained by the costs associated with responding to such feedback. Further research into this area of Web activity is needed.

*Customer Service*: Hotel companies could utilise the Web to provide enhanced customer service. A Web site guide could assist customers in exploring the hotel Web site. A hotel chain could post on its Web site a series of frequently asked questions (FAQs), from which customers might be able to find answers to common queries. Printable property and meeting fact sheets could also be available for customers wishing to make hard copies of on-line information. Customers could be encouraged to book their meeting facilities by the provision of meeting planning worksheets. They could also make on-line requests for hotel brochures, general information and information on meeting facilities.

Furthermore, hotels are also integrating the Web, and the Internet itself, into their products. For example, Inter-Continental Hotels and Resorts offer guests, at one of its international properties, the ability to purchase a card, which allows them one hour of Web surfing via their television remote controls. In May 1997 only approximately half of the hotel chains were offering customer service features. The current survey reveals that 58% are now providing at least one such feature, and of these, 21% have two.

The most significant change is in the number of hotel chains providing meeting scheduling and management facilities. This is now an important feature of many business hotel products, with 29% of hotel chains in the survey offering some form of this service. The range of facilities provided is impressive, with many hotels allowing business customers to book and customise their own meetings venues on-line.

*Public Relation*: The interactive nature of the Web facilitates the building, maintenance and enhancement of relationships between the hotel chains and the influence markets or the general public. A hotel chain could e-mail updates on the company's latest developments to the press. In May 1997, 5.6% of the hotel chains were offering on-line request for photos/information. The current survey reveals that this figure is now 15%. Again, there is growth in the number of hotel chains providing e-mail updates on latest developments, from 0.7% to 3%. The potential of the Web as a public relations tool is gradually being exploited, with 18% of the hotel chains adopting the Web in this way.

*Value-added Service*: Here, a hotel chain could, potentially, provide a currency converter service, weather reports, information on business and travel, news and current affairs, links to travel partners, and links to other Web sites. These features could serve to add value to the customers during their on-line interactions with the hotel chains. The previous study revealed that a large majority of the hotel chains (65%) were not providing any value-added service at all. This has now reduced to less than one third of hotel chains (32%).

The most important growth is in the number of links to business travel partners, which is now 53% and links to other web sites, which is now 58% of those hotels chains in the current survey. Growth can also be seen in the provision of business and travel information, with 38%

offering this feature. News and current affairs mechanisms remain minimal, with only 5% of hotels offering them.

*Web Site for Employees*: Hotel chains could employ the Web as an internal marketing tool to build long-term relationships with its employees. A Web site for the exclusive use of employees could be maintained and employment opportunities within the chain posted. An on-line job application form could facilitate employees in their application process.

The Web site could also serve as an information centre, providing information such as mission statement, company policies, procedures, results, etc. It is evident that the potential of the Web as an internal marketing tool is now being recognised and exploited by many of the hotel chains, with 30% providing a company information centre including employment opportunities, and a further 11% offering on-line job application facilities.

*Channel Members*: The Web offers the hotel chains an interactive communication tool to develop long-term relationships with the channel members. Again, significant growth can be seen in this area, with the proportion of hotels involved increasing from 0.7% in May 1997 to the current figure of 36%.

*Research:* The Web could also facilitate continuous customer data collection and the tracking of customer expectations. Customised or incentivised surveys could be carried out cost-effectively. The finding shows that 11% of the hotel chains now utilise the Web to carry out research, compared with 4.2% in the previous study.

*Additional Features*: The only additional feature found in the current study is the use of the Web to attract franchise interest. The survey revealed that 5% of the hotel chains are using the Web to promote business in this way.

*Multimedia Characteristics*: There is significant use of animation, with 31% of hotel Web sites displaying animated features. The use of music is still underdeveloped, with only 3% of hotel chains using music as part of their Web site development.

Before anyone can write about or discuss e-business, there needs to be a meeting of the minds about what e-business really means. E-business is defined as the transformation of key business processes through the use of Internet technologies. While a lot of attention has been given to externally focused e-business initiatives, in this article we'll explore internally-focused initiatives by taking a look at "e-business from the inside."

The hospitality industry is moving rapidly to the Internet. Most companies are looking at the Internet as a new marketing channel. You can find almost all the hotel chains, management companies, and individual properties on the Internet today. The chains are beginning to accept reservations directly on their web sites and are strongly encouraging customers to book via the Internet. Many chains are also doing some type of auctioning for their unsold rooms.

Most companies have implemented intranets, yet most have not realised their true potential in terms of cost savings, employee productivity, and business effectiveness. Companies are still sharing important business information with their employees by posting, copying articles, and passing information from desk to desk via a routing slip. Very few executives have looked at the impact the web can have on reducing operational costs for the corporation.

### *Cost Reduction*

In today's world, a hotel chain may reduce costs very quickly using the Internet. The Web can be the communication link between the corporate offices and the properties. Cable modems and ADSL/DSL lines are becoming available in many areas, replacing the dedicated phone lines of previous years. These new access and communication tools provide the bandwidth necessary to quickly move critical business information. There are some limitations on where these new devices can be used and when they will be available.

The greatest limitation is the location of the properties and the speed with which the new services reach their areas. As these services become available, hotel companies need to review and adjust their telecommunication strategies. While changing the circuits between corporate headquarters and a property reduces some costs, the real savings comes in reduced communication and administrative costs from using the web as the primary medium to communicate with employees.

In the near future, this communication may include the use of voice over the Web. Some telephone/Web companies are offering this type of service today. Voice over the Web could reduce or eliminate both domestic and international long distance charges—a huge expense for any company. As an added bonus, the types of information that can be disseminated over the Web are virtually limitless: corporate policies, department information, and training to name just a few.

### *Employee Productivity*

*E-mail and Messaging*: The benefits of e-mail are obvious. Electronic messaging connects people who may be geographically dispersed, allowing them to conduct business quickly and efficiently across time zones. It can also be a vehicle for distributing and maintaining the corporate culture through near instantaneous communication of information, stories, and yes, even by supporting the ubiquitous grapevine?

*Web Collaboration*: Tools are now available that make it possible for people to share ideas and collaborate on complex projects by allowing people to participate from geographically distant locations. Team rooms can be established where central copies of documents are kept for easy access by all team members. Everyone contributes to the same copy of the document, which reduces errors and the administrative time needed to copy and distribute documents, receive and incorporate changes, then redistribute. Collaboration tools also facilitate workflow or the movement of information from one user to the next, based on guidelines and rules.

*Training/distance learning*: It's no secret that hotels have high employee turnover, making the time and cost to train and educate new recruits a substantial and continuous investment. Delivering training and other education over the Web will reduce both the cost and time involved and help new hires be productive more quickly.

Sessions can easily be conducted on the Internet for new employee orientations, introducing administrative policies and procedures, conducting technical training on property hardware/software such as POS terminals, PMS system, word processing, spreadsheets, telephone system operation, or explaining new or changed governmental regulations on labour laws, environmental compliance, or foodservice. Travel and program development expenses can be significantly reduced using the Internet as a delivery mechanism.

### *Electronic Human Resources (E-HR)*

This is one area where there can be huge benefits in automating processes and putting them on the Internet. Examples of e-HR applications include the ability to:

— Establish on-line employment applications; publish new hire checklists for managers;

— Allow on-line registration for health insurance; publish

details on insurance benefit options and include searchable lists of approved facilities and physicians;

— Allow employees to register for 401K/pension program participation and permit them to view their accounts and change their investment options on-line;

— Publish bonus information, performance review criteria, organisation charts and reporting chains;

— Publish travel expense policies and approved vendors;

— Allow submission, approval, and on-line lookup of expense reports and their payment status, time sheets, and tracking of vacations, holidays, sick and personal time, and

— Distribute electronic pay statements, which can replace paycheck stubs for employees choosing direct deposit.

Anything that doesn't require a personal presence can be conducted on the Web. With the advent of legally binding digital electronic signatures, even having to personally sign a form will quickly become a quaint custom from the past.

### *Business Effectiveness*

Internet technologies make it possible to do so on a scale unprecedented in history. Web collaboration allows you to apply your best minds to the project at hand, no matter where they may be. Real-time access to critical business information collapses the time needed to take advantage of market opportunities or head off competitive threats. Increased productivity is a natural byproduct of removing administrative and technical obstacles from employees' workflow. Reduced administrative head count and expenses allow precious profits to be directed to areas where they can generate the greatest return for the company. Indeed, using the Web for e-business from the inside may just be an hotelier's secret ingredient for marketplace success.

# Index